Mr + Mrs Perry Spackman

From

Horace + Stella

Wishing you a
Merry Christmas

- 1940 -

Unto the Hills

Those hills at the "Crossroads of the West"—with their sure footings and their refusal to be moved by winds of strange doctrine—hills with their strength, their peace, and their quiet assurance—hills that do not run to and fro, chasing false utopias, following after blind leaders—hills that turn neither to the right hand nor to the left, but stand with calm majesty on rock foundations, no matter what storms may be raging around them.

UNTO THE HILLS

by

Richard L. Evans

HARPER & BROTHERS PUBLISHERS

New York and London

TO ALL THOSE FOR WHOM
LIFE IS A SEARCH

"I will lift up mine eyes unto the hills, from whence cometh my help. My help cometh from the Lord, which made heaven and earth. He will not suffer thy foot to be moved: he that keepeth thee will not slumber."[1]

CONTENTS

FOREWORD

DURING the past years, millions in America, Europe, and the Pacific Islands have been entertained and edified by the Sunday morning broadcasts of the Mormon Tabernacle Choir and Organ, from Temple Square in Salt Lake City.

Of these millions, literally tens of thousands have written in grateful appreciation of the uplifting influence which has come into their lives from the music and the "announcer's 'spoken word' "—which has been so heavily freighted with lofty thought and simple wisdom. These letters have come from all kinds of folk, following all manner of occupations for a livelihood—from high public officials to the most humble daily laborer.

These letter writers have asked to use the "sermonettes" (as they have come to be called) for all kinds of purposes: for texts for church sermons; for reading into the Congressional record; for inclusion in lodge rituals; for professional use by judges, doctors, clergymen, school teachers, and others.

Mostly, however, the writers have wished that they might reread the "sermonettes" for the spiritual comfort and inspiration which were thereby carried into their hearts.

These requests became so multiplied and urgent in their tone, that the commentator and writer, Richard L. Evans, was asked to consider whether he would not be willing to publish in permanent form, such of the "sermonettes" as he might wish to select. After some deliberation, he expressed a willingness to undertake the work, upon the assurance given him that by so doing he would add to the spiritual growth of tens of thousands of his listeners, and would appease, at least in measure, their hunger for righteous counsel and direction.

This volume is the result of that willingness. Its preparation was an added burden to a life already filled, almost to the breaking point, with other church and public duties.

His listeners know the wide range the author's "spoken word" has taken; how deep and constantly true has been his philosophy; how elemental to a righteous life have been his doctrines. He has buttressed his words by the sayings of ancient and modern prophets and by the Divine commands that have come to God's children from the remotest times till now.

For a decade he has had a weekly task to do. It is amazing how little there is of repetition, either in thought or expression, in the whole gamut of his "sermonettes." No other testimony equal to this can be given to the fecundity of his mind and the fertility of his pen.

Tens of thousands have acknowledged the enrichment which has come to their lives by his "spoken word." This volume will enable all these to renew their blessings, and will bring to countless others a refreshing draught of the Master's "living water" to slake their thirst for things spiritual in this barren waste of modern materialism.

J. REUBEN CLARK, Jr.

Salt Lake City, Utah

AUTHOR'S PREFACE

For nearly ten years these brief "sermonettes," as radio listeners have chosen to call them, have been "talked off" on a dictaphone, under the pressure of a relentless weekly broadcast schedule. During this time many listeners have inquired as to their source, their procurability, their originality.

As to originality—that is, of course, a relative term. The words and the phrases belong to the author insofar as he is aware—except where there has been a borrowing from scripture, in which case the debt is acknowledged. As to originality of thought—well, they represent the author's convictions, the source of which is that common heritage of truth available to all who will be partakers of it.

It is the author's belief that the millions who have listened this past decade to the Tabernacle broadcasts over Radio Station KSL and the nation-wide networks of the National Broadcasting Company and the Columbia Broadcasting System, successively, have done so for these fundamental reasons: because they enjoy good music sincerely interpreted; because humankind instinctively respond to truth; and because the modern day in which we live demands brevity—and these "sermonettes," it is fondly believed, combine fundamental truth with brevity of expression.

This volume contains those comments most widely requested.

RICHARD L. EVANS

Salt Lake City, Utah

ACKNOWLEDGMENTS

DEBTS for services rendered are here acknowledged:

To the Tabernacle Choir, its organists, conductors, officers, and its more than three hundred members, who, with their predecessors, have sung and rehearsed for nearly a century past, without monetary compensation of any kind, and who have performed each week on nationwide networks for more than ten years, continuously, paid only by the love of singing and the joy of rendering service. This organization has been at once the background, the inspiration, and the necessity for these writings. This program, "presenting music and the spoken word from the Crossroads of the West," is said to be the oldest continuously presented, nationwide sustaining program in American radio history.

To President Heber J. Grant and his counselors, J. Reuben Clark, Jr., and David O. McKay, for their interest, criticism, and confidence.

To Dr. John A. Widtsoe for his untiring encouragement and earnest helpfulness, and, also, on the same counts, to Earl J. Glade, Executive Vice-President of Radio Station KSL, whose forward-looking policies were responsible for placing the Tabernacle Choir program on nationwide networks a decade ago; and, to T. Albert Hooper.

To Marba C. Josephson, William Mulder, Elizabeth Moffitt, D. H. Vincent, and other members of the staffs of the *Improvement Era* and Radio Station KSL, for criticism and technical assistance.

And, especially, to those unnumbered listeners

throughout the United States, Canada, and beyond the seas, whose letters, whose personal visits, whose requests and comments and appreciation, have called forth this collection.

I. Time and Its Passing

"My days are swifter than
a weaver's shuttle."[2]

1. SPEED AND DIRECTION

In our mad struggle to get somewhere, it is to be hoped that we may not lose sight of where it is we want to get. Our day has come to place great emphasis on speed and efficiency, but let it be borne in mind that these things are not virtues in and of themselves, but are useful only when applied with wisdom and purpose. What good is speed if it takes us more quickly to the wrong destination? What good is efficiency if it is applied to a machine or a system of degradation and destruction? A human life is an eternal thing, and no matter how much we attempt to crowd into it, we can live it no faster than time passes. And it is well to remember, even in this day of speed, that enduring qualities are worth infinitely more than getting nowhere fast. It is not the rapidity with which a man travels that gives us concern; it is the destination he has in view.

❊ ❊ ❊

Since the evening and the morning of the first day, the most relentless and most constant occurrence of man's existence is the passing of time and the changes wrought by it. Threescore and ten is the number of man's allotted years, so says the word of scripture. To some of us much less, to some of us more, but to all of us, time has its certain ending. In the hour of happiness and in the company of cherished friends we would stay its march, but onward speeds it on its way. For a time of sorrow and for a day of loneliness we would hasten its step, but it plods its measured course, and the sweep of the tide, the lowering of the sands, the tick of

3

the clock, and the lengthening of shadows mean that life has journeyed so far on its measured course, that another moment of the present has become a moment of the present has become a moment of the past, never to return, except in memory, and never to be lived again except as the record of eternity may sometime be reviewed. If it is evil that awaits us, time's passing haunts the souls of men and makes cowards of the brave. But if we live unto a day of good, each daybreak is welcomed for the labor and the living that it brings, and each evening for the promise of its rest. And for those who have steadfastly pursued the ways of life in the right direction, the evening of mortality means that "they shall rest from all their labors here, and shall continue their works"[3] where dwell the righteous departed.

❊ ❊ ❊

WHILE travelling in a strange land, Jacob awoke one night to exclaim with wonder: "Surely the Lord is in this place; and I knew it not."[4] Jacob was no more startled by his discovery than have been many men since his time—men who have attempted to run away from life, from conscience, and from the Lord, and, who, even though they have travelled fast and far, have found that wherever they may be, life and conscience and the Lord are, in the words of Jacob, "in this place," also. Some men who have felt they have had things to run away from have not been so foolish as to take a journey into a far country—they have been more foolish: even so foolish as to remove themselves, by their own hands, from the presence of men. But even there they will find, according to the word of the Lord which fails not, that God is in that place also, that conscience goes with them, and that life and all of its problems and mistakes must be faced, even

4

in that realm in which men find themselves beyond the grave. And so, lest any man decide to take a far journey in this world or into any other, let him remember now, so that he may not be surprised later, that life is as long as eternity, and that no man may travel faster or farther than his conscience, nor beyond the realm of accountability to the Lord God his Father in Heaven. Since life is a thing of everlasting duration, it would seem to be better to solve its problems here, rather than to carry them unsolved into the hereafter.

2. PERSPECTIVE

WHILE the journey down through the years may seem long, in memory the years are short, and we may look back upon them with great things and small assuming their true perspective, and with all obstructing pettiness cleared away from the backward view. Some things we might have done differently, but now that is all in the past, and the past is as changeless as truth itself. Neither God nor man may alter the record of what has gone before. And since the lessons of the past cannot improve the past, utterly wasted are they unless they improve the present, and determine the future. God grant that it may be so. It is a sorry man who has made a mistake, but a foolish man who does not profit by his error.

❊ ❊ ❊

TIME has a way of casting a halo over the past. The long look back gives credence to things at which the present scoffs. We may believe of another century what we could never believe of our own, and that the God of Heaven guided a people in ancient times seems plausible even to many who would deny such guidance today.

❊ ❊ ❊

As WE find ourselves growing older, and as cherished friends depart upon the last long journey, there seem to grow among us a changing sense of values and a deeper discrimination between things worth while and things of only passing worth. The closer comes the journey's end, the more highly we esteem character and the less we grapple for riches. The nearer draws the parting day, the more deeply we cherish the peace of an untroubled conscience and the less we value the superficial approval of men.

※ ※ ※

As WE walk haltingly through life, repeating its mistakes and learning its costly lessons, we may sometimes be led to wonder why it is not given us to know more than we know. It would seem reasonable to suppose that we could do better if we were granted greater perspective—if we had more intimate knowledge of what has gone before and what is yet to come, back beyond the reaches of our memory and forward beyond the penetration of our foresight. But such thoughts are dispelled when we contemplate what does frequently happen when knowledge without judgment and power without conscience are found in the hands of a man. Such thoughts dissolve themselves when we realize that even now we have pushed the frontiers of abstract learning and material advancement far beyond our spiritual and social progress and have thereby upset many delicate balances for which we are paying a price. In the light of such things, it is easy to understand that the plan designed by the Creator is the one best suited to the good of man. And it would seem to be the course of wisdom to seek no greater power or dominion than we can justify by the use we have made of the facts and forces which are already in our possession.

※ ※ ※

WE SEE so many things that we do not comprehend! We hear so many things that do not penetrate our intellects! We feel so many things that seem to lie beyond our powers of understanding! The familiarity of our surroundings has made us impervious to much of the significant reality that is intimately close to our lives. Unthinkingly we pass up eloquent sermons in commonplace things and in the daily lives of the men and women with whom we live. Would that we could be more thoughtfully observant, in accord with the scriptural exhortation: "Get wisdom, get understanding: forget it not. . . . Wisdom is the principal thing; therefore get wisdom: and with all thy getting get understanding."[5]

❊ ❊ ❊

PERCHANCE, as the days crowd in upon us, we are too close to life to see it well. Sometimes in judging all things by our own height, pettiness assumes magnitude because of its proximity, while the distant object, which is really great, seems not so to be, because it does not shadow us night and day. God grant us an enlarged perspective!—so that as the weeks and the months and the years roll by, we shall behold with open eyes those things which are greater than our own stature.

❊ ❊ ❊

SEPARATION by time or by space, for most of us, gives to many things a seeming value, which, were they nearer, perhaps would not be so highly regarded. The squalor of a distant city is often a place of glamour to those who are far removed from it. Nor does a man usually take his rightful place in the annals of history until those who knew his human weaknesses have likewise faded from the scene. To revere ancient and distant things and respect the contributions of the past is a thing to be commended. We would also that we could safely

8

glorify the present and fairly judge the greatness of the men and things with whom we live today.

❋ ❋ ❋

IN OUR own thoughts we are sometimes guilty of attaching great importance to some people and comparatively little importance to countless millions of others. In a limited sense this is justifiable. People whose lives most closely affect our own lives are important to us. But in a larger sense, in the great scheme of things, everyone who walks the ways of life is important. It does not matter if he belong to some other family, or live in another neighborhood, or move in a different social circle from ours, or think different thoughts, or subscribe to different standards, or speak a different language. The worth of souls is great in the sight of God, and since the Lord has not placed a limited value on the souls of men, men accordingly have no right to do so. And we have learned one of life's greatest lessons—one of its most far-reaching and vital lessons—when we can look upon every man who walks the ways of the world—the ailing, the infirm, the unfortunate—the cripple and the beggar—of every creed and clime and caste—and know, regardless of how we find him or how we see him through our eyes, that he is a significant, eternal being, a very child of God, even though he may appear to be of little consequence from our limited perspective. When all men learn this, we shall be on our way toward greater things to come.

❋ ❋ ❋

TO BELONG wholly to the past is a futile thing. The past can never live again, except in memory. Its shadow is with us yet, but its reality belongs to the ages that never return. Man goes forward, eternally forward, but never back. That is why the past is at once so remorseful and remorseless. And that is why the present is so all-important—because the present is continually becoming part of the changeless past.

❀ ❀ ❀

LET neither the glories of the past nor the promises of the future cast their dimming shadows over this ever-present moment in which we live.

❀ ❀ ❀

"They become blinded and understand not the things which are prepared for them."[6]

THE SPIRIT OF HOLIDAY COMMERCIALISM

SOMETHING should be said concerning that spirit which seems to have grown up around all of our holidays—specifically, the spirit of commercialism. If a holiday is to be perpetuated from year to year, it seems reasonable to suppose that it should be perpetuated for the spirit and purpose which brought it into being. But in our generation a price tag has been placed upon many of our ideals and sentiments and memorials. The material gift has dominated Christmas rather than the spirit of giving, and frenzied shopping days have driven its deeper meaning far into the background. Easter has become a day for new clothes and other outward observations. Mother's Day likewise has taken on its materialistic aspects and in many places has become a day for a brief outward demonstration of that thoughtfulness which should be shown the mothers of men throughout all the year. And so we might continue down the list of those festivals and holidays and special occasions which we formally observe by closing banks and schools and other scenes of activity, and by special markings on the calendar, but which we have largely sold out to purposes and interests for which they were never intended. Perhaps we should read again that New Testament account wherein the Savior drove the money changers from the temple and cleansed His Father's house—and with this example before us set about to do likewise for those traditional days which were

11

conceived with a deep and sacred purpose—all to the end that our children may have an awareness that the Fourth of July is more than fireworks and that Christmas is more than Santa Claus.

❋ ❋ ❋

EASTER

ON THIS day, observed as the Sabbath of Easter, un-numbered millions of men and women throughout the world remember with gratitude the resurrection and triumph of Him whose influence has been more persistently felt than anyone who ever crossed the pages of history. From Him we reckon time. To Him we look for counsel. Him we seek for wisdom and understanding when the journey we are travel-ing together becomes difficult. To Him we look for eternal life and the promise that "whatever prin-ciple of intelligence we attain unto in this life, it will rise with us in the resurrection. And if a person gains more knowledge and intelligence in this life through his diligence and obedience than another, he will have so much the advantage in the world to come."[7] Thus it is recorded; thus it is promised by the Son of God.

❋ ❋ ❋

MOTHER'S DAY

THOUGHTFUL attention on Mother's Day is the due of every mother, but no true mother ever lived who would not rather have her son grow to useful man-hood, loving integrity, cherishing truth, and living in righteousness, than she would have all of the demonstrative once-a-year evidences of affection that could be heaped upon her. To honor his mother with the highest of all honor, a man must realize his greatest usefulness in life, must render the most worthy service of which he is capable, must cherish truth, love virtue, esteem character, and must uphold, on all occasions, the highest ideals and principles of which he has any knowledge.

❊ ❊ ❊

MEMORIAL DAY

We are increasingly aware that death is a time of remorse only because the living are bereaved and not because the dead have ceased to live. Life goes on undaunted by such meetings and partings because always there is that certain knowledge that every parting will be followed by another meeting at another time and in another place, and because always there is that assurance of the eternal permanence of the human soul. With such an approach to death, Memorial Day becomes more a time of honored remembrance and less a time of unsatisfied grief.

❊ ❊ ❊

INDEPENDENCE DAY

It is greatly to be desired that the fireworks and festivities and running to and fro should not completely overshadow the deeper significance of the Fourth of July to all who enjoy life in the land of the free. And perhaps the greatest lesson that could be remembered is that freedom is not a tangible commodity that may be locked away in a vault and preserved without effort for all time—rather freedom is a highly perishable thing that must be nurtured, cherished, and preserved at whatever cost. From out of the record of scripture we read: "whatsoever a man soweth, that shall he also reap."[8] And if we sow with indifference, with idleness, with dis-

13

content, with animosity of brother to brother, with corruption, with arrogant selfishness, we shall awake some morning to observe too late the shackles with which we have bound ourselves. No blessing of the Lord God is guaranteed to men save according to their obedience. And the price of freedom in a free land is eternal vigilance, regard for law, and uncorrupt living.

* * *

ARMISTICE DAY

MORE than a score of years ago, the world called a halt to what, up to that time, had been its greatest mistake. The end of conflict came only after millions had killed other millions, and after men had destroyed each other's most cherished possessions, both of the spirit and of material substance. We still pay for that God-forbidden desolation and destruction. We shall continue to pay in more ways than we know for generations yet to come. And again we have with us wars and rumors of wars, for which we cannot blame a new generation, because there are still so many among us who remember vividly that other conflict and who know full well all of the horror of it. No truer words were ever spoken than that like begets like. Greed is the breeder of greed. With power grows a lust for power. A blow brings a blow in return. Competition is the sire of competition, and armaments call for more armaments. And thus we find ourselves to be the unwilling victims of many vicious circles. It is still true also that a soft answer turneth away wrath—but where shall we go to find a soft answer? It is small comfort to know that they who live by the sword shall die by the sword—but at least it is true. It is as John beheld from the place of his exile: "He that leadeth into captivity shall go into captivity: He that killeth with the sword must be killed with the sword. . . . If any man have an ear, let him hear."[9] There is a way out. May the Lord God our Father help men to see it before they become blinded by the hatefulness of the thing that is before us.

❀ ❀ ❀

THANKSGIVING

THE season of harvest and thanksgiving makes men more thoughtful. It is the time when the world takes inventory of the fruits of its labors and looks upon the increase with an appraising eye. At this season some of us find that the Lord has blessed us with a bounteous harvest. Some of us find that we have labored long and diligently and are rewarded with but a meager reaping. Some of us find that we have lived in indolence and that now we must eat of the fruits of other men's labors, and for such un-earned bread we find little appetite. Others find that they have much increase of this world's goods, but have paid too great a price for the things they garner. All of us would do well to look back and evaluate the fruits of our labors with a true and fearless sense of what is worthless and what is of great worth.

❀ ❀ ❀

MORE than three centuries ago a Pilgrim colony reached the shores of America. They had wandered far and given much to obtain freedom of conscience. In the generations that followed, the heroic achievements of this nation have justified the sacrifices of the early Fathers and of all the patriots who have followed them. Through divine Providence truth-

15

loving men and women have reared a nation mighty and respected in all the world—a land of plenty and a land that has a future as well as a past. If, in this day, and in this land, there be those who are discontented, such discontent is of man's own devising and comes not of the Lord. The earth is the Lord's and the fullness thereof, and of that fullness men may be partakers only insofar as they give obedience to the laws of righteousness. There is at hand a fullness of things spiritual and of things material if we will but set our houses in order and prepare ourselves for the enjoyment of all good things which life holds for those who live it faithfully and well.

❀ ❀ ❀

CHRISTMAS

AT THIS season of giving, may we include among our gifts things more priceless than can be bought with money and more lasting than can be fashioned by the hands of men. If we can give hope to a neighbor whose hope in an eternal future has been dimmed by a much too worldly present, we shall have given that which is of more worth than any gift that could be conveyed in colored wrappings. If we can give to those who live in doubt an unshakable belief in those eternal standards of truth which will yet remain unchanged next Christmas, or a thousand years hence, we shall have given that which brings peace to the hearts of men—even that which Jesus the Christ brought into the world on that memorable night from which we reckon time.

❀ ❀ ❀

CHRISTMAS marks the time of year when faith, hope, and charity seem to penetrate more warmly the hearts of men, and when tolerance and brotherly kindness become something more than abstract principles, if only for a short season. It is the time when a perplexed and somewhat troubled world becomes more thoughtful and men become, for the moment at least, their better selves, and when burdened nations look toward brighter things even with that hope which found a waiting world on that night when angels sang "Glory to God in the highest, and on earth peace, good will toward men."

※ ※ ※

AT THIS season of remembering, may it be granted that with our remembrance of the past we may not forget the urgent needs of the present, in which a restless generation seeks for guidance, for understanding, for truth, and for changeless standards in a changing world.

※ ※ ※

MANY notable figures have walked across the stage of mortality and have tried by their words and their deeds to leave their impressions upon their own generation and the ages to follow. Many of these great ones of earth have been benefactors of mankind. Others have been tyrants. Some have excelled in the arts and in the things that men fashion with their hands. Some have relieved human suffering. Some have merely sought to regiment their fellow men and mold them to their own misguided purposes. Some have been remembered and others have been forgotten. But of all these, none has entered into the fibre and being of all human thought and worship as has Jesus of Nazareth, who came out of a lowly country, who spoke few words of which we have record, but who left His stamp upon the world for all time, and the endless hereafter to follow.

※ ※ ※

17

CHRISTMAS means divers things to various peoples. It is a season of mingled moods and many customs. It means the exchange of greetings of good will. It means holly and ivy, and lights and tinsel, and abundant feasting. It means giving and receiving and merry-making, and worship of Him who is the Son of God and the Savior of mankind. And from the prophets to whom it has been given to know, even more surely than by faith, the burden of their message is this: "And now, after the many testimonies which have been given of him, this is the testimony, last of all, which we give of him: That he lives! For we saw him, even on the right hand of God; and we heard the voice bearing record that he is the Only Begotten of the Father— That by him, and through him, and of him, the worlds are and were created, and the inhabitants thereof are begotten sons and daughters unto God."[10]

❋ ❋ ❋

THOUGHTS ON A PASSING YEAR

WE MAKE much of seasons and of holidays and of fleeting occasions. We make much of the year's ending and the year's beginning, as though the stroke of midnight, by some strange alchemy, transformed the world and all our lives and changed the picture of the universe. But with all the changing times and seasons there are in the heavens those things which change not and are eternal. These are the things that cause the world to keep its balance and cause men to return to moderation, despite the strange doctrines, false teachings, and fantastic schemes that trouble this age and generation.

❋ ❋ ❋

WE MEN of earth, who grow old together as the

18

hours and the days pass us by, find ourselves again at that season which marks the year's ending and the year's beginning. With mingled feelings we watch the deeds and thoughts of another cycle of days become part of the record of the past. As the year closes, there is high spirit mingled with deep thought, and short-sighted hilarity keeping company with solemn retrospection.

❋ ❋ ❋

As we close the book of the year that has passed and open a new ledger for the accounts of another part of life, may it not be forgotten that the creditors of eternity are more inexorable than Scrooge or the proverbial Shylock. The books may be closed, but the accounts must still be paid. In the eternal journey of the human soul, there is no act of bankruptcy which may quickly free us of the shackles of our debts to life, and the judgments in which the Lord God deals do not become outlawed by any Statute of Limitations. Man may settle his obligations for a few cents on the dollar here, but the coin of the realm hereafter is not subject to discount, and every debt will be paid, both for good and for ill. With the reality of such facts in mind it is good to open the New Year.

❋ ❋ ❋

Until a season changes, or a day passes into night, or a year closes, we are almost unaware of the passing of time. But with the beginning and ending of definite periods on the calendar, we are shocked into an awareness that time moves quickly and relentlessly on its endless way, and we wonder what we have done with it and what we have learned both within our own lives and within the broader scope of our generation and century. It is apparent

19

that we have learned many important things and that we have failed to learn some which are of greatest importance. We have learned to travel something less than four hundred miles an hour on land and somewhere near that speed in the air. We have learned to move about under the seas on missions of great destruction. We have learned to prolong the span of life with our medical science and to sweep a whole populace off the face of the earth with our warfare. We have learned to bring down music and speech from the apparent nothingness of the heavens above. We have learned to counterfeit the products of nature—to make rubber, to make silk, to make plastics which in some respects prove to be superior to the natural products. We have learned to sustain the beat of the heart long after it has been removed from a living organism. We have learned to treat and to cure many diseases —but not to change the human frailties and social practices that cause their growth and their spread. We have learned to weigh and to measure and to analyze the stars, to raise a plant without soil, to harness energy that does the work of a million slaves; and we have learned to bring before our very eyes the living, moving image of a friend who may be many miles away. Having learned so much, does it not seem a strange thing that men collectively have not learned to live at peace with their neighbors and have not found the secret of an abiding and untroubled happiness within themselves? Does it not seem a strange thing that having learned so completely the importance of observing the laws of science to the smallest detail in order to bring about a given result, we seem not to have learned to observe the laws of human happiness found both in the record of our experience and in the revealed word of God? For this purpose the year now passed is hopelessly gone, but the year that lies broadly before us *could* see the ideals of mankind well within reach if we would sincerely give ourselves to the human and eternal values to the same degree that we have given allegiance to our material progress, which, without its moral and spiritual counterpart, is a curse and not a blessing.

❀ ❀ ❀

THIS is the season of a dying year—the end of a journey for some and the start of a journey for others. But it seems to matter not who shall pass today—tomorrow life will continue much the same as it has moved today—with new names, new faces, new ways of saying old things, but always with the same old plots and situations and the same changeless fundamentals of truth that live from everlasting to everlasting, despite the coming and the going of the years.

❀ ❀ ❀

MEN fear the passing of time only when it has been misspent. They who have used well their allotment of hours and days and years, glory in each moment's achievement and welcome the coming of each year's beginning. And to thoughtful men it becomes apparent that things as fine as truth and courage, loyalty and friendship, and intelligence were not created nor achieved to be done away with at the end of any year or age. Life and its endless realities go on despite the changing of the date we post upon our calendars, and men continue with their searchings and their findings ceaselessly down through the ages.

❀ ❀ ❀

IT IS wisdom on the part of the Creator that the

21

year should have its ending and its beginning, that it should be divided into seasons and days and hours, that the days should be divided into lightness and darkness, that sleep may restore the weary, that rest may soothe the sorrowing, that daybreak may give hope to the unhopeful. The year has been made to close that men may, in a measure, bury and leave with the past the error of their lives and begin anew to build for that which is to come—but eternal man continues to be what past years have made him and continues to become only as great and good and wise as the sum of all he has been and done, despite all resolutions and good intentions for times yet to come.

❊ ❊ ❊

WHAT visions of the past recall to memory is beyond the power of man to alter or efface. Time gone is time gone. Life lived is life lived. Now the task in hand is so to spend our hours today that tomorrow may welcome its memories.

❊ ❊ ❊

THE resolve to live better in the future than we have done in the past is a commendable step in the right direction, but the resolve to live better in the present than we have done in the past is by far the higher determination. The future belongs to tomorrow. The past belongs to the realm of things that never return, but today we live, and today becomes an indelible part of us tomorrow.

❊ ❊ ❊

WE LIVE in a world of waiting. Few men there are but who are waiting for something or someone. We wait for loved ones to return. We wait for dreams to come true and ambitions to be realized. We wait for the time of sorrow to pass and for the time of joy to come again. We wait for the harvest to reward our summers and for spring to break our winters. We wait for justice to take its course, for truth to triumph, and for righteousness to cover the earth. It is well to live in a world that awaits the passing of the years and the events they bring, but it is good also to live in a world that does those things which will make its waiting shorter.

❈ ❈ ❈

FOR those who live in waiting, the hours drag—but the years speed quickly by. For those who bide the coming of great events, time is a spendthrift that makes men grow old quickly—but slowly moves the progress of the world.

❈ ❈ ❈

WE HERE face the changeless record of our own past and the unwritten record of our own future.

II. "O the Vainness, and the Frailties, and the Foolishness of Men!"

"When they are learned they think they are wise."[11]

1. SOME PERSISTENT FOLLIES

THIS matter of imparting confidential information to others with the understanding that the knowledge so given is not to be carried further is a prevalent practice that calls for comment. What right have I to suppose that my friend will keep a secret that I could not keep? How can I know but that my friend has another friend to whom he will tell my secret and whom he will also swear to secrecy? And so the news travels from friend to an ever-widening circle of friends—always in confidence! That secret which I cannot keep I have no right to expect another to keep. And if I betray a confidence, I may certainly expect to hear that my friend and my friend's friend have also betrayed that confidence. It is well not to speak that which should not be spoken, else the world will soon hear of it—because so many people have so many confidential friends!

❊ ❊ ❊

WITHOUT meaning to do so we have in some measure become victims of a system of publicity and sensational news reporting that ofttimes makes public heroes of our public enemies, martyrs of our criminals, and makes the best news out of the worst phases of our living. Once let a man defy all of the laws, all of the conventions, all of the decencies of society, and his name and face and deeds and words are known to all of us. He becomes a public figure and a kind of glamour attaches itself to him in spite of anything that we seem to be able to do. And when he finds himself facing justice, a certain amount of sentimental support rises up in his defense. This is true both of those who commit acts of violence and of those who are guilty of deeds of dishonesty with respect to public or private trust. It seems almost at times to have reached that stage wherein a man feels that he should be apologetic for not having won any greater distinction than living life quietly, honestly meeting all his obligations, doing his best to observe the laws of men and of God, and "going about doing good." Such a man has no news value, and yet he is the reason why we have, fundamentally, a great and good country to live in. It would be refreshing to see a headline dedicated to that man. But he gets his satisfactions from living in other and happier ways.

❊ ❊ ❊

WE HAVE paid our respects to many varieties of human ills, but there is one cankering practice, not peculiar to any time or place, that causes our thoughts, if not our words, to rise in eloquent protest. We have reference to that brand of whispering which travels like a wind-swept fire from ear to ear, and destroys, without conscience, the good name of a man, the reputation of an institution, the integrity of a nation, or whatever it chooses to blight and wither. To shout base things in the market place, to print a libelous statement, or to bear false witness in violation of the commandments of God and men are crimes traceable to their source and for which there is due punishment. But he who carries his unholy wares on the breath of a whisper which sweeps from lip to lip, and which, by its innuendo, suggests more than it says, is of all men most despicable. And because of our own receptiveness to gossip, and our own frail eagerness to be the first to tell something, we enlist ourselves in the spread of half-spoken untruth oftener than we should care to admit. May heaven keep a man and his possessions from the blight of those who whisper at his back.

* * *

THE memory of man is short and convenient. When he is warmly protected, he may forget the penetration of bitter coldness, and that other men are cold. When he is abundantly well fed, he may forget the gnawing pangs of hunger. When he is in the company of affectionate and understanding friends, he may forget that there is much loneliness, and that even he could find himself without a friend. When he is prosperous, he may forget that chance and numerous other things within the realm of possibility may alter the fortunes of men with relentless unconcern. When he is at peace, he may forget that the price of peace is tolerance, understanding, brotherly kindness, and an active sense of honest justice. When life deals easily with him, he may forget that the difference between everlasting happiness and certain regret lies in doing the will and keeping the commandments of the Lord God.

* * *

THERE is a prevalent attitude of mind that causes most people to speak of the troubles of the world as though the world were something apart from them and for which they have no responsibility. It is a fact that many of us expect other men to do the improving, others to make the sacrifices, others to take the leadership, others to run the risks. We expect our neighbor to be public-spirited while we serve self-interest. We look to others to resist the temptations to which we ourselves have yielded, or would, under similar circumstances, yield. Some other man, some other family, some other community must practice altruism—but we—we have our own to look after and must find the easy and immediate way of doing it. If the world has its troubles, it is because we are not what our neighbors think we should be and because our neighbors, unfortunately, are just as human as we are—because we expect a better performance from someone else than we are prepared or willing to give ourselves. It reminds one so forcibly of that utterance of eloquent simplicity in the Sermon on the Mount: "And why beholdest thou the mote that is in thy brother's eye, but considerest not the beam that is in thine own eye?"[12] Let us not deceive ourselves on this score: why should we be surprised to discover that other men are no better than are we ourselves?

❊ ❊ ❊

MEN who think they pursue their lives independently of all other men and independently of all outside forces are as foolish as the seaman who thinks he pilots his ship alone, when he steers by the stars in the heavens and takes his bearings from maps and instruments that centuries and generations have produced. No man is a law unto himself. His mother bears him; families, friends, and society rear him from infancy; other men teach him, make the clothes he wears, provide the food he eats, and run the world he lives in; and God who is in heaven crosses his path with influences and impressions. Let no man play the fool and glory in his own self-sufficiency, for no man lives who is self-sufficient.

❊ ❊ ❊

EACH generation is impressed with its own originality and feels that its own accomplishments are greater than any contribution that the past has made. Men and women, individually, are inclined to follow the same rule. Thoughts occur to us which we think are original. How disillusioning to find that someone has thought the same thing and written it down a hundred or a thousand years ago! How damaging to our vanity to find that some things that have been done in the past have never been duplicated or equalled in the present!

❀ ❀ ❀

In an age of much learning we marvel that men are so careful to observe the laws of truth in some things and so careless in their disregard for them in others. The miracles of material advancement that daily rise before our eyes are possible because thoughtful, searching scholars have discovered natural laws, and have meticulously observed and applied those laws to bring forth wonders heretofore undreamed of. But these very men, so brilliant in some respects, are frequently found disregarding many other laws of life with seeming unconcern for consequences. The situation calls to mind that text of scripture uttered many centuries ago, but fitting in its application even unto a modern day: "O the vainness, and the frailties, and the foolishness of men! When they are learned they think they are wise, and they hearken not unto the counsel of God, for they set it aside, supposing they know of themselves, wherefore, their wisdom is foolishness and it profiteth them not. And they shall perish. But to be learned is good if they hearken unto the counsels of God."[13]

❀ ❀ ❀

On one of those numerous occasions when Jesus of Nazareth paid His quiet but trenchant respects

31

to His accusers and would-be destroyers, He said: "I have made a man every whit whole."[14] It would be well-nigh impossible to express in fewer words the ultimate purpose of all the Creator's planning, and of all of man's righteous endeavor than in these: to make men every whit whole. To feed a man's body and leave his spirit hungry falls short of attaining the scheme of creation. To give a man bread in exchange for his fundamental rights and liberties of thought, speech, and action is something less than making a man "every whit whole." To force a man where his conviction does not lead him, to induce him to exchange a quiet conscience for a material advantage, or to raise him where his effort will not carry him nor his industry sustain him is something less than making a man "every whit whole," and therefore falls short of serving the ultimate purposes of God and the ultimate good of man.

❀ ❀ ❀

Perchance there has been an all too ready willingness for assigning God to His Heaven and man to his earth. Perchance there has been an all too hasty disposition for relegating religion to the church and living to the world.

❀ ❀ ❀

It matters not by what names we choose to call our vices and our virtues; they remain what they are and what they always have been before men and in the sight of God. In the modern scheme of things if we choose to call licentiousness by the flattering title of broadmindedness, licentiousness nevertheless continues to be licentiousness. If we decide to apply the name liberalism to despotism and if we call bondage freedom it matters little, because despotism and bondage continue to be what they are and what they always have been. If our generation is pleased to call virtue and honesty old-fashioned relics of a gone and forgotten day, that does not make of virtue and honesty anything different from what they have always been, and it does not lessen our need for them, though we pretend to have found more convenient and desirable substitutes. If there be some in our generation who wish to consider faith in a living God and the certainty of His judgments an outworn superstition, again the fact is not altered that God still lives, that His judgments are sure, and that all men will one day be brought before Him to render an account of themselves. In short, the modern disposition to re-label and re-classify and re-evaluate the very foundations upon which civilization stands, in no way changes the facts of life or the laws of living.

❋ ❋ ❋

As WE look back upon the record of those generations which have gone before, and see, with an impersonal perspective, their mistakes, their failures, and their successes, we are inclined to wonder why we must go over the same ground again and again and again. With thousands of years of history behind us, and the record of its lessons plainly written before us, there seem to be those among us who still suppose that something can be had for nothing, that outward force is protection against our inward weaknesses, that injustice may forever go unchallenged, and that disregard for law may be indulged without the penalties falling upon us. History has repeated itself and has taught the folly of these things to each generation, but the lessons do not seem to have been carried down very successfully from father to son.

❊ ❊ ❊

Some of us find ourselves at times in an attitude of resentment or envy toward the apparent prosperity and well-being of those whose seeming success and good fortune have been achieved by practices which conform neither to the laws of men nor of God. Particularly to young and immature minds, that such things are permitted to continue is sometimes taken as justification for departing from straight ways and following crooked paths on the supposition that if evil may be committed with impunity and with profit by some, why should others not have their share of the spoils thus gotten—all of which goes to prove that the world has not changed much these many centuries and that human nature is still the most constant thing in all the universe. For even in his day, the ancient Preacher was shedding the light of his wisdom upon the situation when he said: "Because sentence against an evil work is not executed speedily, therefore the heart of the sons of men is fully set in them to do evil. Though a sinner do evil an hundred times, and his days be prolonged, yet surely I know that it shall be well with them that fear God . . . But it shall not be well with the wicked."[15]

❊ ❊ ❊

For the benefit of our confidence in mankind, generally, perhaps it should be said that comparatively few men deliberately set out upon a course of lawlessness, sin, and unconventional living. Such careers are built step by step with one error leading to another, and one lie calling for a thousand more to make it seem to be true. And having once set out

34

upon such a course, the return is as difficult as fighting back through closed doors which open readily in one direction but open with difficulty in the other. And therein lies the danger of the currently popular and flippant spirit of "trying anything once." It is such false philosophies that make first indiscretions easy and second violations easier, even unto the forming of habits. It has been long since the writer of Proverbs uttered this advice, but the wisdom of his words has not diminished: "Ponder the path of thy feet, and let all thy ways be established. Turn not to the right hand nor to the left: remove thy foot from evil."[16]

❈ ❈ ❈

THERE is nothing in history that would justify any age or any civilization in feeling self-sufficient or overly secure. The past constantly reminds us that there is no civilization so great that it cannot be disintegrated by the indiscreet latitudes in which great civilizations presume to indulge. The past reminds us as often as we turn to its record that there is no nation so self-sufficient that it cannot be defeated by its own inordinate confidence. The record of the past reminds us as often as we turn back its pages that there is no generation so secure that it cannot be brought to sorrow and calamity by its own ignoring of the fundamental laws of truth and right.

2. THE FEARS OF MEN

THE men of this generation are haunted by many fears. We fear the headlines and the by-lines. We distrust good news and quake because of bad news. We hear of apprehension over crop shortages and consternation because the yields are too abundant. We are fearful of the evils of prosperity, and we shrink from the perils of adversity. In a time of peace we are fearful lest it cannot endure, and we shudder as a time of war approaches. Surely we look out upon such a day as that spoken of by the prophets who saw that men's hearts should fail them and that they should run to and fro upon the earth. And it is but a short time until we shall realize, if we do not already do so, that the only protection lies in the integrity of men, the love of neighbor for neighbor, and a close approach to God. Until we bring ourselves to this understanding, our living may be described in these words of Job: "When I lie down, I say, When shall I arise, and the night be gone? and I am full of tossings to and fro unto the dawning of the day."[17]

❅ ❅ ❅

MEN fear the hour of loneliness, but the greatest loneliness is not the loneliness of solitude. They who live in the midst of thousands of their own fellow creatures are ofttimes more lonely than the hermit who dwells at peace with his thoughts. They who jostle with the thoughtless crowds on city streets are ofttimes more lonely than they who are far from the thronging crowd. The number of people we see has little to do with our loneliness, but the companions of our thoughts and the warmth of our hearts toward the things and people around us determine the loneliness we feel.

* * *

MANY of us strive in vain for things that we believe we want, but more of us strive not knowing what we want. More fear and discontent are caused by the uncertainty that comes from within than by the external obstacles that stand between us and the objectives we strive to achieve.

* * *

THE traditional economic definitions of value and security seem of late to have lost much of their meaning. The traditional standards of physical protection and safety seem also to be outdated. In a bygone generation it was a comparatively simple matter to lock one's treasures away from the grasp of thieves or to build a wall against the onslaught of enemies. But such hazards are more subtle and less tangible than once they were. In our day, when good and evil have both taken on refinements, a man's treasure can dwindle from him without any hand having touched it, no matter where he locks it up and no matter how well he guards it, merely by the depreciation of its trading value in a world where such manipulations have become possible and common. Outmoded are the strong box, the castle moat, and the city wall. Attack from above and within, and attack with the subtler weapons of propaganda, whisperings, and noisy oratory have made the strong-armed physical defenses cumbersome things of the past. It all reminds us of that Psalm wherein it is written: "Except the Lord keep the city, the watchman waketh but in vain."[18]

* * *

It seems to have become popular to speak of what is wrong with the world. The elements of negation, complaint, criticism, and fear seem to have cornered the headlines and the by-lines. This in itself would not be serious if we could be assured that the process of tearing down were being more than offset by the process of rebuilding, but concerning this point our minds are not at ease. We are fearful lest many who have been successful in attracting attention to themselves and who now find themselves in high places have no very good idea concerning what they are going to put in the place of the things they are discarding nor how they will rebuild the faith and courage and trust and industry of the people in whom they have sowed the seeds of doubt, distrust, indolence, and fear.

❧ ❧ ❧

In all nations and among all peoples one of the most frequent questions is this: In what shall I place my trust? The query is being spoken in numberless different ways, and where it does not actually reach the lips of men, it finds deep place in their troubled hearts. It is part of human experience that when a man finds his material and intellectual world tumbling down upon his head he seeks refuge in those eternal verities which seem for the moment, perhaps, to be less tangible, but which are, in fact, the only constant values in all the universe. It is as the Lord expressed it through one of His prophets: "Who art thou, that thou shouldest be afraid of a man . . . and forgettest the Lord thy maker?"[19]

❧ ❧ ❧

"And the Spirit of God moved upon the face of

38

the waters. And God said, Let there be light: and there was light. And God saw the light, that it was good: and God divided the light from the darkness. And God called the light Day, and the darkness he called Night. And the evening and the morning were the first day."[20] And since the evening and the morning of the first day, true and thoughtful men have cherished light and all that it symbolizes, and have done their work in the fullness of the day, so ordering their lives that the coming of night with its darkness holds for them no fears, because they have no accuser from within or from without. But they who have worked in darkness find that darkness has become their master rather than their protector, and they live their lives amidst all its terrors.

❈ ❈ ❈

So SURE and unfailing is the certainty with which remorse follows our misdoings, it is greatly to be wondered that men persist in disregarding the rules of life. Perhaps there may be some who would ask what there is to restrain us or to induce us to do otherwise—certainly not threats or fear of physical punishment. Fear of physical punishment never made a good man in any land in any age. The most relentless penalties of a man's misdeeds are things less tangible and more terrible: the accusation that comes from within; the dull heaviness of a heart that knows it is not clean; the dogged pursuit of a conscience that allows no peace and no surcease; the heaviness of spirit that comes with the disapproval of a Heavenly Father whose children all men are—these are the real price a man pays for his misdeeds, as David of Israel testified with heartbreaking conviction when he cried out to his Eternal Father: "Hide thy face from my sins, and blot out all mine iniquities. Create in me a clean heart, O God; and renew a right spirit within me."[21]

＊ ＊ ＊

ONE of the greatest common desires of men is the desire for security. For our happiness it is not enough to know that we are well fed today. We must know that we shall be well fed tomorrow. While we live always in the present, we project our thinking into the future, and what, in reality, could be a very happy present situation, may be converted into sorrow or fear by the prospect of coming misfortune. It is not enough to know that our storehouses are full—if next year's increase is placed in jeopardy, this year's harvest is not tasteful to us, in anticipation of that which is to come. So universal is our desire for security, that men have often been known to barter their fundamental rights for the promise of it, and therein lie the strength of despots and the ease with which they have always placed themselves in power. Too great a price has often been paid, even for our comfort. He who promises us bread, whether it be his to give or not, asks too much when in return we must yield the right to worship as we choose, to speak as we choose, to teach our children as we choose, and to live as free men. Especially is this true since no power can guarantee us our security except the Lord God, and He only in accordance with our observance of those laws and commandments which always have and always will govern the universe and all that it encompasses.

＊ ＊ ＊

"And all things shall be in commotion; and surely, men's hearts shall fail them; for fear shall come upon all people."[22]

3. DOUBT AND BELIEF

THERE are many things that men deny for lack of understanding. We doubt what we cannot see. We discredit those things which lie beyond our powers of comprehension, but the world and the universe go on despite our unbelief. The fact that limited intelligence has misconceived a fundamental truth does not invalidate that truth. The fact that human capacity for understanding is greatly restricted does not restrict the powers beyond our understanding— and this is our protection against our own ignorance, for which we thank God, who rules the heavens and the earth and all that in them is.

❋ ❋ ❋

WE HEAR much said concerning doubt. In an age of skepticism and general unbelief, men are inclined to doubt many things. In an age when so much that is false finds itself intermingled with so much that is truth, men in some quarters are inclined to look upon doubt as a virtue and to doubt even those things which are well supported as to their truth. Indeed, there are many who, for the license that it gives them, profess to doubt even the fundamentals upon which civilization rests. Lest we have any misunderstandings about the true nature of doubt, may we say that in and of itself it is neither a vice nor a virtue. It may be good or it may be bad. If it exists for its own sake and perpetuates itself, it is a thing of evil. But if it leads to a search for knowledge and removes itself, it may be a wholesome influence. An honest doubter looks for an answer to his question. But an insincere doubter stubbornly harbors his unbelief for its own sake, shunning the enlightenment that would cast it out. The logical conclusion of honest doubt is understanding. Either a proposition is true or it is false. When we have determined which, we have removed doubt. In short, that doubt which immediately leads to inquiry, and thereby removes itself, is wholesome doubt. But that doubt which feeds and grows upon itself, and, with stubborn indolence, breeds more doubt, is wrong. To doubt may be a step on the path of knowledge, but never the destination of that road. By the open inquiry of an honest mind doubt may be removed even in a world where many have become smug with their doubts.

※ ※ ※

CONCERNING all things, some men disagree. What thousands steadfastly believe to be true, other thousands are equally sure is false. It may be safely said that there are no two men who believe and disbelieve all things alike. This being true, the great virtue of tolerance, each for his neighbor, and the great need for it, are readily understandable. But even so, there are some things that lie in the realm of fundamental truth, concerning which there may be no conjecture. These things we must some day all be brought to believe.

※ ※ ※

EXCEPT for the faith of men in the orderly procedure of natural things, life could not go on as it does. We believe that a time of harvest will follow a time of planting; that honest work will find its recompense; that good will be returned for good; that the dawn of day follows the darkness of night. These and so many more we must believe, that it is but a small step further to believe that there is eternal purpose in it all, and that the intelligence of God orders it all, for the Lord "hath given a law unto all things, by which they move in their times and their seasons; . . . The earth rolls upon her wings, and the sun giveth his light by day, and the moon giveth her light by night, and the stars also give their light, as they roll upon their wings in their glory, in the midst of the power of God . . . Behold, all these are kingdoms, and any man who hath seen any or the least of these hath seen God moving in his majesty and power."[23]

❋ ❋ ❋

AMONG so-called "unbelievers," religion and the God to whom it looks as the Ruler of the universe are disposed of with a wave of the hand. But remove these things in reality from the lives of men and women, and behold an emptiness, an irreparable void. They who would take away without replacing do so at their own peril and at the peril of all whom they convince by their deception.

❋ ❋ ❋

THE skeptic avows his disbelief yet lives in a world that belief has built. He destroys the foundation, but seeks shelter in the building. He eats food that an unknown hand has prepared and believes in its wholesomeness. He plows and plants and believes that the rains will come. He harvests and stores his surplus, and believes that a time of winter will show the wisdom of his labors. The skeptic believes with the rest of the world, despite his avowed disbelief.

❋ ❋ ❋

"WHO is this that darkeneth counsel by words without knowledge? . . . Have the gates of death been opened unto thee? or hast thou seen the doors of the shadow of death? . . . Where is the way where light dwelleth? and as for darkness, where is the place thereof? . . . Canst thou lift up thy voice to the clouds, that abundance of waters may cover thee? Canst thou send lightnings, that they may go, and say unto thee, Here we are? Who hath put wisdom in the inward parts? or who hath given understanding to the heart?"[24] If there be any who scoff at faith, who disbelieve Omnipotence, who would reduce to mechanistic chance the well-ordered laws of the Ruler of heaven and earth, let these questions be put to them, even as they were asked of Job.

❋ ❋ ❋

WE ARE sometimes reminded that there is a prevalent cynicism which prides itself upon disbelieving those things which God-fearing men and women for centuries have cherished as truth. Knowing this, perchance it were well to keep in mind that every age and every civilization has produced its quota of cynics. The cynics come and go, but truth and the fundamental virtues continue, changeless, undaunted, everlasting, unmindful of the weak dissenting chorus which would rob us of our belief in eternal verities, were it possible to do so.

❋ ❋ ❋

IN GENERAL it may be said that men believe what they want to believe. If we desire to think ill of an acquaintance, ungrounded rumor is ofttimes accepted as fact even in the face of contrary evidence. If we desire to think well of a friend, facts which might detract from our good opinion of him are discounted, even in the face of reliable counter testimony. Occasionally men may be convinced against their will, but not often. Since, in the main, we

44

believe only what we desire to believe, should not our desire be to believe only truth—always truth— even in the face of a seemingly more attractive false-hood?

❋ ❋ ❋

For much of our knowledge in this world we must accept the testimony of others. As laymen, we can neither prove nor disprove the theories and the findings of the scientist. Indeed, many propositions which are given the dignity of scientific fact cannot be reproduced in the laboratory by the man of science himself, and yet we accept them because of our belief in the integrity and superior knowledge of the trained scientific intellect. The man of religion asks no more than that—no more than simply belief in those things which, though they now seem incapable of proof to some, are nevertheless true and harmonious with whatever knowledge men possess.

4. CHRONIC ILLS AND NEGLECTED CURES

WHATEVER the ills of the world may be, we become daily more convinced that the problem is not so much one of administering the proper medicine as it is of making a correct diagnosis. Too many social physicians are administering antidotes for maladies the nature of which they know not, neither do they understand. The problem is not one of want, nor of plenty, nor of power, nor of weakness, nor of race, nor of creed, nor of divers political philosophies. The nations that have little escape it not; the nations that have much escape it not. The vexation of prosperity is no less great than the vexation of poverty. It is a question of man's inhumanity to man, a question of right and wrong as regards the fundamentals of living, and until men master themselves, all of the would-be cure-alls are merely opiates of relief. But despite all this, an element of hopefulness we find anciently expressed: "If thou seest the oppression . . . and violent perverting of judgment and justice . . . marvel not at the matter: for he that is higher than the highest regardeth; and there be higher than they. . . . Let us hear the conclusion of the whole matter: Fear God, and keep his commandments: for this is the whole duty of man."[25]

❁ ❁ ❁

THE limiting factor in building a more perfect world is neither the earth nor the things of earth, neither laws, nor ideals, nor principles, nor a

Utopian plan. All these things we have. The limiting factor is men and their ways—because they know better than they do; because principle is overshadowed by self-interest; because laws are thought to serve as substitutes for individual integrity; because the seeming remoteness of heaven is forgotten for the short-lived pleasures of earth. And so our lives fall short of the ideal that lies within our reach, and for our troubles we are led to blame all manner of remote things when in reality the responsibility lies uncomfortably close to the daily thinking and living of each of us.

❊ ❊ ❊

FROM the record of scripture and of history we are forced to conclude that there has always been a generous quantity of this thing called "human nature." How like today are these words with which the Lord described His people in another day: "They were slow to hearken unto the voice of the Lord their God; therefore, the Lord their God is slow to hearken unto their prayers, to answer them in the day of their trouble. In the day of their peace they esteemed lightly my counsel; but, in the day of their trouble, of necessity they feel after me."[26]

❊ ❊ ❊

WE LIVE in a day when the needs of the world are much discussed. The views of economists, the plans of statesmen, the promises of politicians—many are prescribing; many are assuming the role of physician. May we suggest, simply, but without apology: more trust, less intrigue; more humility, less vain conceit; more love, less pretense; more service, less self; more concern about what God wishes, less intrusion of our short-sighted whims. It is a humble

47

formula, but it has worked and, if tried anew, will work again.

❀ ❀ ❀

IT IS quite natural for us to wish for power to adjust the apparent inequalities and injustices we see around us. But perhaps such endeavor on our part would carry with it an all too grave responsibility. We men!—with our short-sighted wisdom we might do more far-reaching injustices in setting right what seems to us to be wrong. We cannot see the thoughts that lie behind the facial mask. We cannot see the real intent buried deep within the heart. Perhaps, then, it were just as well to let Providence guide the destinies of the world, and to co-operate with that Providence, rather than to assume for ourselves the role of Creator and Judge.

❀ ❀ ❀

AND while we are about our reading, may we sometimes look beyond that which is currently written and refresh ourselves, away from the confusion of conflicting modern views, with the wisdom and the beauty and the satisfying words of the sacred record—the Bible.

❀ ❀ ❀

IN AN age of complexity and sophistication, anything as direct and satisfyingly simple as the Ten Commandments stands out in refreshing relief. Sometimes we forget them. They are still good for all men. One of them reads: "Remember the sabbath day, to keep it holy. Six days shalt thou labour, and do all thy work: But the seventh day is the sabbath of the Lord thy God: In it thou shalt not do any work."[27] No wisdom or philosophy of the moderns has yet displaced the fundamental precepts

48

of the Decalogue to the happiness of man or to the glory of God.

* * *

IT WAS not a thing of chance, but an outgrowth of untold ages of experience with human nature that brought among those commandments which the Lord gave to Moses the injunction: "Thou shalt not covet . . . any thing that is thy neighbour's."[28] And by this word to all men, it is not meant that we may not admire what our neighbor has, and seek by our own industry to produce things of like worth. The earth holds plenty for all, and all men are deserving of the rewards of their own industry. The cause for censure comes when we grasp for that which rightfully belongs to another or for that which we ourselves have not paid by our own industry, thrift, and sacrifice, whether it be a tangible property or a mode of life. Even this one commandment, could it be observed in a twentieth-century world, would relieve many stresses among men and among nations and would bring peace and good will to dwell where there are now distrust and avarice.

* * *

WHENEVER we wish to say a thing better than we can say it, with greater authority than we can give it, and in language stronger and more fearless than our own half-courage is wont to use, we derive much satisfaction from turning to the word of scripture, and finding there expressed thoughts of our own in the trenchant and incontrovertible language of others. To this deposit of truth well spoken, we turn for such thoughts as these: "Wealth gotten by vanity shall be diminished: but he that gathereth by labour shall increase."[29] And again: "He that tilleth his land shall have plenty of bread; but he that followeth after vain persons shall have poverty enough."[30] And yet again: "I have been young, and now am old; yet have I not seen the righteous forsaken, nor his seed begging bread."[31]

✤ ✤ ✤

WE WHO look to the lessons of the past find, somewhat to our comfort and somewhat to our sorrow, that other men at other times have paid the price of their follies, and have been forced to turn again to the fundamentals of right living as the only solution for the many ills that they have heaped upon their own heads. Throughout Old Testament history it was the constant cry of the prophets: "Jerusalem, O, turn thee to the Lord." And for brief respite, Jerusalem did at times turn to the Lord, but peace led her to prosperity; prosperity to vanity; and vanity to affliction, poverty, and humility, and a turning again to things of righteousness. It is a familiar cycle, true in the life of most men, and of every nation.

✤ ✤ ✤

IT HAS been anciently said: "Thou shalt love thy neighbor as thyself." This thing is difficult to do in a modern world, even as it was anciently. Most of us bear resentment and ardent dislike for some of the men and women whom the Lord has seen fit to let live at the same time and in the same place as we. But for our own enjoyment of life and peace of mind, it were well for us to rid ourselves of all such resentment, even though it be with great and conscious effort, because even though we were permitted to dwell on earth far beyond the normal age of man, we should probably never find a time or a place in which there were not some people around us whom we could dislike if we but chose to do so. Strange as it may seem, obeying the injunction to love our neighbors as ourselves will probably be of far greater value to us than to our neighbors, because neighbors come and go, but always we live with ourselves and our own thoughts, whether they be thoughts of dislike and resentment or thoughts of kindness and tolerance.

❈ ❈ ❈

OUR vital concerns are not so much with things as with men. Things—material things—are in and of themselves neither good nor bad. It is man's use of them that makes them one or the other. The same airplane that rushes life-saving serums to an area of epidemic may drop life-destroying bombs on helpless civilians. The automobile that rushes a physician on an errand of life may carry an intoxicated driver on a mission of death. The same flood waters that destroy homes may, under the control of man, sustain life. The rule is true even of the virtues. The same sincerity which leads a man to promote a good end, may, in a twisted brain, lead another man to pursue fanatically a bad cause. And so, neither material possessions nor abstract virtues determine the goodness or the badness of the world in which we live. This is determined by men and the use they make of all the things that come into their lives. If we wish a better world, we should begin to make it so by working with men rather than with physical properties or abstract virtues.

❈ ❈ ❈

BEFORE we seek new cures for old ills, were it not well to try some of the old cures that have proved effective in times past, but which are sometimes forgotten today? There are enough precepts in scripture, enough laws on the statute books, from olden times until now, to cure all of the world's complaints many times over, if men would but give belief and obedience. To multiply fantastic schemes is useless. To create new cure-alls is folly. The old cures will still work when men are ready to apply them. Such old-fashioned things as heeding the commandments of the Lord, dealing in honor with men, and maintaining an example of virtue and integrity in our homes will still do for any people what they have always done whenever they have been observed in the past.

❋ ❋ ❋

EVERY age and every land has had its wanderers— its seekers after better things. This day also has need of its pilgrims and its pioneers—not so much to discover and settle strange lands, but to explore and classify strange doctrines. The intellectual maze of theory, falsity, and fact cries earnestly for sound thinking—for the clearing of muddled modern minds—while untruth and near-truth strive vainly to discredit truth and reality. We need today, as the world has always needed, straight-thinking men with the courage of their convictions. And, thanks be to God, we still have them, if we but let their voices be heard above the roar of confusion.

III. Freedom and Restraint

"Have ye forgotten the captivity of our fathers?"[32]

THERE is some modern disposition to suppose that the means justifies the end, no matter how drastic or deceptive that means may be. Superficially, and in isolated cases, this may sometimes be true, but it is never true where fundamental principles are compromised, or where truth is ignored, or where human liberties are set aside. And of those who would sacrifice human rights to achieve allegedly desirable ends, it should be known that "while they promise . . . liberty, they themselves are the servants of corruption: for of whom a man is overcome, of the same is he brought in bondage."[33]

❋ ❋ ❋

ALL of the ills that men complain of have their origin sometime, somewhere, in a broken law. Man's right to think and act independently does not transcend his obligation to law. If it were so, chaos would rule and reign. Freedom is the child of obedience to law, while bondage is born of opposition to law. Here or hereafter, men may progress only insofar as they give recognition and observance to this great underlying principle, for "there is a law, irrevocably decreed in heaven before the foundations of this world, upon which all blessings are predicated— And when we obtain any blessing from God, it is by obedience to that law upon which it is predicated."[34]

❋ ❋ ❋

"BEHOLD, this is a choice land, and whatsoever nation shall possess it shall be free from bondage, and from captivity, and from all other nations under heaven, if they will but serve the God of the land, who is Jesus Christ."[35] For this assurance, and for the faith of our fathers, we are thankful. For their reverence, we bless their memories. For their devotion to ideals, regardless of expediency, politics, or personal ambition, we are grateful. For their integrity in holding the good of country and countrymen above self-perpetuation in office and power, we revere them. The freedom for which they lived and died is a symbol of that freedom which is the birthright of all men—that freedom of which the Lord spoke when He said: "I, the Lord God, make you free, therefore ye are free indeed; and the law also maketh you free. Nevertheless, when the wicked rule the people mourn. Wherefore, honest men and wise men should be sought for diligently, and good men and wise men ye should observe to uphold; otherwise whatsoever is less than these cometh of evil."[36] May this land in which we live never be found without the leadership of such men in its hour of need.

❊ ❊ ❊

As we look back upon the history of human rights, we are forced to conclude that this thing called liberty is not a modern invention, but a fundamental requisite to human happiness. It was written in olden times: "Abide ye in the liberty wherewith ye are made free; entangle not yourselves in sin, but let your hands be clean"[37]—clean from the rust of idleness, from the corrosion of inactivity, from the decay of indolence—clean from the tarnish of other men's goods, or from the taint of reaching after other men's goods. These are among the elements that go into the making of liberty. The past would make it seem that men love liberty more than life, for so many have died to bring it to us; and, perchance, many others would yet follow their example, if such dark days should ever return.

❀ ❀ ❀

IT MAY be that the world is more troubled of late, or it may be that our troubles seem to be multiplied by modern means of communication, whereby we know not only those things which disturb our own peace, but also the major misfortunes of all other men and nations. This breaking down of isolation, this growing oneness of world interest, intensifies our burden and tightens the strain of our living and thinking. But there is comfort, in looking back, to know that all the would-be usurpers of the rights of free men have come and gone, while truth has persisted. Freedom has repeatedly raised herself from the dust, and fundamental human rights have emerged again and again. Thus it may ever be while free men have breath and while despots have unrestrained ambitions.

❀ ❀ ❀

LIBERTY is of more than one kind and character. There is the liberty of environment that comes from living in peace and understanding, in tolerance and respect, with our neighbors, those who are next door and even unto those who are farthest removed from us. And then there is the liberty that comes from within, that is attained by each man in his heart and soul when he learns to declare himself free of error, imaginary fears, and wrong-doings.

❀ ❀ ❀

WE ARE so constantly mindful of our material heritage, that perhaps something should be said

57

concerning the intangible heritage to which we are all heir. We have a heritage of liberty, paid for by the patriots of generations past. It comes to us without price, but it will not remain with us except as we pay for it with an unceasing vigilance and by obedience to those laws and principles by which liberty is guaranteed to all men. We have a heritage that assures us freedom of worship, freedom of speech, a voice in our own regulation, and the right to live our lives as individuals and not as part of a regimented group. But whenever we indifferently or foolishly suppose that these intangible guarantees, once having been bought and paid for, shall remain forever with us, regardless of our individual responsibility or lack of responsibility toward them and their maintenance, they shall vanish from us overnight, as quietly and surely as the darkness steals upon us. And let this not be forgotten whenever we as a people are tempted to barter for whatever expediency or efficiency or temporary advantage, any element of our dearly-won and quickly-perishable heritage. Let it be asked of us continually and of generations yet unborn, even as it was asked of an ancient people: "Have ye forgotten the captivity of our fathers?"[38]

❀ ❀ ❀

IN THIS day of many laws and much lawlessness, when even the fundamental structure of human rights and liberties is sometimes called into question, perhaps it were well to refer to words of wise counsel on this subject which have been preserved through the years: "That which is governed by law is also preserved by law. . . . That which breaketh a law, and abideth not by law, but seeketh to become a law unto itself, . . . cannot be sanctified by law, neither by mercy, justice, nor judgment."[39]

As it is with men so also with communities and nations. As the world regards its laws, those of God and men, so will its peace and safety be.

✽ ✽ ✽

It seems that men have been inclined to look for unusual manifestations from the Lord, and in looking for spectacular signs have forgotten that the Lord's way is the way of law and order, the way of the ceaseless movement in the heavens, of the regularity of the seasons, the way of a boy growing into manhood, the way of a tree's flowering and of the sun's ripening. The Lord God does not need to speak to men in great voice (although He may do so at His choosing), for He has planted in them a voice of conscience and inspiration which, unless it has been suppressed or tampered with, speaks as truly as truth itself. On this thought, there comes this text: "And, behold, the Lord passed by, and a great and strong wind rent the mountains, and brake in pieces the rocks before the Lord; but the Lord was not in the wind: and after the wind an earthquake; but the Lord was not in the earthquake. . . . And after the earthquake a fire; but the Lord was not in the fire: and after the fire a still small voice."[40] And in that still small voice onward came the Lord.

✽ ✽ ✽

"The Constitution of the United States is a glorious standard; it is founded in the wisdom of God; it is a heavenly banner; it is to all those who are privileged with the sweets of its liberty, like the cooling shades and refreshing waters of a great rock in a thirsty and weary land. It is like a great tree under whose branches men from every clime can be shielded from the burning rays of the sun."[41]

59

And it was established by Almighty Providence at "the hands of wise men whom I [the Lord God] raised up unto this very purpose."[42] And such belief is made no less valid by the fact that there be some who, in their short-sighted expediency, would wish to make it seem that it were not so.

❀ ❀ ❀

CONCERNING laws and governments there is a declaration of belief accepted by many thoughtful men with the same unquestioning force as are the words of the ancient prophets. It reads: "We believe that governments were instituted of God for the benefit of man; and that he holds men accountable for their acts in relation to them, both in making laws and administering them, for the good and safety of society. We believe that no government can exist in peace, except such laws are framed and held inviolate as will secure to each individual the free exercise of conscience, the right and control of property, and the protection of life."[43]

❀ ❀ ❀

HEREIN lies the protection of all people—that they shall place their trust not in the technicalities of the statute book but in the stewardship of wise and honest men.

2. ALL THINGS IN MODERATION

WHEN men cite the fundamental instincts of human nature in justification for their misdeeds, they wander far afield from truth and human experience. The forces of human nature, in common with all other things immutable, must be controlled before they are useful. There is no more justification for letting our basic human instincts run wild and free than there is for letting our gardens and our fields run wild and free. There is no more rightful reason for letting our desires and impulses burst forth unrestrained than there is for letting the turbulent flood waters break through dams and destroy human life and property. Intelligent control and thoughtful restraint within our own being, as well as among the things that surround us, is the only way of life wisdom and experience justify.

❀ ❀ ❀

IT MAY be safely said without fear of contradiction that any practice in life may be carried to an extreme; that any aim may be pursued to an absurdity. Moderation in all things is the most sure way of happiness, contentment, and ultimate achievement. The extremes of life in any direction are generally responsible for the maladjustments that cause our discontent and give rise to many incongruities in a world which, however good to live in, might yet be infinitely better.

❀ ❀ ❀

NOT everything is outworn simply because it is old. Not everything is good simply because it is new.

The old order changes and the new order fills our lives, but they who live wisely cling fervently to all that was truth in the old and to all that is truth in the new.

❋ ❋ ❋

THE rewards of living a life of thoughtful restraint are not confined to a remote hereafter, but are present here and now. It is, even as scripture records: "He who doeth the works of righteousness shall receive his reward, even peace in this world, and eternal life in the world to come."[44]

❋ ❋ ❋

THERE are some things that must be learned by all men who wish to live effectively and at peace with themselves and with the world. There are more than can be mentioned here, but notable among them are these: It is wisdom to be moderate before the infirmities of age force moderation upon us. It is wisdom to be thrifty before the sharp pinch of need makes itself unpleasantly felt by prodigal ways of living. It is wisdom to cultivate friends before the help of friends is urgently needed. It is wise to be prayerful before nothing but a prayer can comfort or help us.

❋ ❋ ❋

THE things of which men speak when they find themselves together are a revelation of the depth of soul and quality of character that lie behind the facial mask. It is pleasant to pass the time of day commenting lightly on the weather and on the events of the social calendar. But it is also good to balance such conversation with a tempering consideration of those fundamental values which undergird our very lives. No man should spend his days with trivial and transitory things to the exclusion of eternal realities.

❊ ❊ ❊

EACH generation seems to discover the virtues and the vices of all the generations that have lived before. But strangely enough, there is something that keeps us in a sort of balance: No one ever quite forsakes the good; no one ever quite forsakes the evil; and life goes on with its queer and contradicting tendencies toward right and wrong, some day, we hope, to triumph toward the right to the exclusion of all things else.

❊ ❊ ❊

IN THE day in which we live, as in generations gone by, there are two extremes of thought striving for supremacy, neither of which must be allowed to become supreme. One faction supposes that age itself is a virtue, and that time can give the dignity of fact to things that are less than fact. Those who thus contend fail to perceive that an error, even though it has become traditional, is still an error and that time alone cannot make truth of anything that is less than truth. Another school there is that believes that old things are outworn without consideration as to whether they be true or false—that there is virtue in change and in newness for the sake of change and novelty themselves, and that, as a matter of principle, the established order should be done away. But all such fail to perceive that that which is new may as easily be wrong as a falsehood that is old. The conclusion of the matter is this: Truth has nothing to do with age. Truth is ageless. And neither the cobwebs of tradition nor the glitter of novelty can make or unmake a truth nor give the dignity of truth to that which is inherently

63

false. This lesson our generation has need to learn, before we cling to old errors on the one hand, or before we grasp too eagerly for worthless changes on the other.

❀ ❀ ❀

IN LIFE, as in the arts, symmetry is a thing to be cherished. To follow the pursuit of material accumulation to the exclusion of things spiritual presents as distorted a picture as an unfinished work of art; nor may such a life be of more use or credit to the designer than is the unbalanced work of the artist.

❀ ❀ ❀

IT IS well to know the zest for work without making gain your God; to know the worth-while contributions of the past without becoming enslaved to error, custom, and tradition; to know the joy of companionship without fearing solitude; to know the destiny of man and the purposes of God without becoming self-righteous and too far removed from the world.

❀ ❀ ❀

"GOD doth not walk in crooked paths, neither doth he turn to the right hand nor to the left, neither doth he vary from that which he hath said, therefore his paths are straight, and his course is one eternal round."[45] And since God turns neither to the right hand nor to the left, it is well that men should do likewise in all the ways of life.

3. MAN'S RIGHT TO CHOOSE

No MIRACLE or quack scheme can lift any nation or civilization above its own desire and honest effort, and no power, human or divine, can force men to inward righteousness in this land, or any other. It is a principle of divine government, established in the heavens before time began, that men shall determine the course of their own lives and take the consequences therefor. Such is the grave responsibility of all men, and none there is who may escape the right of choice—with all of its obligations—for "good and evil have come before all men," and "it is given unto you to judge, that ye may know good from evil."[46]

❊ ❊ ❊

THERE is much said concerning "we the people." No one is more misquoted; no one is more flagrantly misinterpreted; there is no one whose thoughts and words and desires and interests are more warped and twisted for the convenience of the moment than are those of "we the people." This brings us to the question: Who are "we the people"?—and the obvious answer: You and I and our neighbors. And the world in which we live is no better than we are. Our thoughts and our lives, and our secret and open acts, and secret and open desires are the reasons for whatever condition the world is in, whether we like it or not, because that indefinite "they" of whom we speak when we say "Why don't 'they' do something about it?" is simply "we the people"—you, and I, and our neighbors. Concerning "we the people," an ancient American prophet once delivered a pertinent message. He said, among other things: "It is not common that the voice of the people desireth anything contrary to that which is right; but it is common for the lesser part of the people to desire that which is not right."[47] And he continued: "And if the time comes that the voice of the people doth choose iniquity, then is the time that the judgments of God will come upon you . . . then is the time he will visit you with great destruction."[47] And so it seems that "we the people" have, before God and our fellow men, a grave responsibility—you, and I, and our neighbors.

❋ ❋ ❋

THE evils of the world we see about us are chargeable more to stupidity, ignorance, and weakness than to a deliberate choice of wickedness. Most of the errors of men are committed either because they know no better or because they are too weak or too stupidly indifferent to live as well as they know. The Lord, through His prophets, has made some allowances for blind mistakes when He said: "Where there is no law given there is no punishment."[48] But He has also said: "It is impossible for a man to be saved in ignorance,"[49] which means that there must yet come a day of greater enlightenment and of living in accordance with that enlightenment, before the race of men can rise to those heights of godliness for which it is destined.

❋ ❋ ❋

TO RAISE a society of people to artificial standards by coercion and regimentation is the direst sham, because there is no way of permanently lifting men higher than their own intelligence, their own desires—or higher than their own efforts and industry

66

will carry them. If we wish to save any people, we must teach them to save themselves. If we insist on elevating them by external force, they will revert to their own level as soon as the pressure has been removed. This was the fundamental issue when war raged in heaven, when Lucifer offered to force all men to salvation. Thereupon that other Son of God, Jesus, the Christ, offered to show all men the way of salvation and teach them to strive toward it of their own desire and effort.

❀ ❀ ❀

THERE is a widely accepted legal maxim to the effect that ignorance of the law is no defense. And yet, as most of us go through life, we ask to be excused for many things by reason of our ignorance, and we are prone to say to ourselves: "We would do better if we knew better but how may we acquire wisdom and how may we surely know the right from the wrong." Let it be assumed that most of us have a sincere desire to do the right thing and that our tragedies and failures come not so much from lack of willingness as from lack of wisdom. Even making allowance for this, the very fact of our permitting ourselves to remain in ignorance while we are within constant reach of the source of all wisdom, is something to be accounted for. It was Robert Browning who said: "Ignorance is not innocence, but sin."[50] And from another source: "Ignorance, when voluntary, is criminal, and a man may be properly charged with that evil which he neglected or refused to learn how to prevent."[51] To state the proposition in another way, we have for our guidance the accumulated record of human experience: the spoken and written thoughts of the great and the wise; the sacred and inspired words of our various scriptures; an active voice of

67

conscience, which is reliable if we have not tampered with it; and an approach through prayer to the God and Father of us all, in response to which we may receive the promptings of the "still, small voice." And by all of these, the fundamentals of life are indelibly and unmistakably defined. They do not change from generation to generation even though our regard for them may change. With all this before us, why should we ask or expect to be excused for our ignorance or our lack of wisdom. And if we still insist that our ignorance should be allowed as an excuse for our misdeeds, we shall surely be called upon to answer for that greater guilt by which we permitted ourselves willfully to remain ignorant in spite of all the ever-present sources of wisdom that lie constantly before us. The real answer lies not in a scarcity of wisdom, but in our own lack of will and determination to acquire and apply our hearts unto wisdom.

❊ ❊ ❊

CONSIDERING that the fundamentals of right living have been known to men for so long, it is to be marveled that we make the same mistakes so many times and so readily forget the lessons of the past. Considering that the rewards of obedience and the penalties of disobedience to the laws of men and of God have so often been seen before our very eyes, it is to be wondered that men should so often hesitate in their choices in life and should so often make the wrong choices. It is a wise man who seeks wisdom. But it is a blessed man, who, having found it, forsakes all else to pattern his life in accordance therewith.

❊ ❊ ❊

SOMETIMES we speak of the powers of evil and temp-

68

tation and of our own acts of weakness as though they were things apart from us and beyond our power to alter or control. When such thoughts present themselves, remember that man cannot disclaim responsibility for anything which he does knowingly by speaking of the forces or circumstances which prompted it as being things apart from him. He who is blinded by error is yet accountable for that departure from the straight road of life whereby he permitted blindness to overtake him. No man can destroy his own faculties, then be excused for his failure when he needs them.

* * *

No DOUBT we are deprived of much that we might enjoy in this world because so many of us are so willing to let others create ideas and make opportunities for us. The Lord, our Creator, would not have given men the ability to think and act independently if He had not expected us to use our own free will and initiative to think useful thoughts and bring about constructive works. It is written: "For behold, it is not meet that I should command in all things; for he that is compelled in all things, the same is a slothful and not a wise servant; wherefore he receiveth no reward. Verily I say, men should be anxiously engaged in a good cause, and do many things of their own free will, and bring to pass much righteousness; For the power is in them, wherein they are agents unto themselves. And inasmuch as men do good they shall in nowise lose their reward. But he that doeth not anything until he is commanded, and receiveth a commandment with doubtful heart, and keepeth it with slothfulness, the same is damned."[52] No man is justified in expecting the world to lay its treasures at his feet. For the good things of earth and for the enjoyment of them we must use the best powers of mind and matter and spirit of which we have any knowledge or control.

❊ ❊ ❊

THERE may be some advantages in seeking out and becoming familiar with the negative and untoward side of life, but such advantages are far outweighed by the disadvantages. If we remember all that we see, then were it not wise to see only those things that would be good to remember. If we remember all that we hear, then were it not wise to hear only those things that we should be gratified to recall. To do this, it may be granted, is not always possible. Sordid things sometimes cross our paths in spite of our desire to avoid them. But, on the other hand, there are people who are all too ready to seek out sordid things, and they stand in danger of having sordidness become a part of them, for men become the image of the world wherein they choose to dwell.

❊ ❊ ❊

SOCIETY can punish men for their misdeeds; it can destroy them for capital offenses; it can incarcerate them for infractions of law, and intimidate them with a show of strength. But society can never force men to be good unless they choose to be good. Even when one is forced to an outward semblance of goodness, he may still think basely and destroy his own soul with mental offenses. No man was ever forced to goodness, and, even if he were, it would be no credit to him. The goodness which upbuilds the souls of men has its origin within.

❊ ❊ ❊

THE power of association is relentless in its consistency. Virtue seeks after virtue; hate breeds hate;

selfishness is the reward of selfishness. And the man of evil thoughts and actions in the presence of truth and righteousness would be no more comfortable than would be he of coarse speech and awkward mien in the courts of royalty. The wicked can never dwell at ease with the good, here or hereafter, because between them is little in common. Men must therefore choose the society in which they wish to live, and live lives consistent with their choice.

❋ ❋ ❋

WHAT man is there among us who shall say what is of most worth in life? Some there are who choose to barter for the things that material wealth can buy. Some there are who seek for power as the thing most highly to be cherished. Some esteem freedom and independence of thought and action as the thing of greatest worth. And some who live among us choose to gamble all chances of lasting happiness against foolish and momentary pleasures. Since we who walk the ways of life cannot agree each with his brother as to what is most to be valued, may we not then agree to the wisdom of accepting the judgment of the Lord, our Creator, and on His appraisement take unto ourselves those things which are eternal—those things which a man may take with him when he departs hence, and which bring unregretful happiness here and hereafter?

❋ ❋ ❋

IT WAS the immortal Shakespeare who gave to one of his characters a question that has since been asked times without number: "What's in a name?" The answer, of course, is: Nothing, unless the name fits and accords with the thing to which it is given. Modern men—and perhaps the ancients, too—are often guilty of attempting to secure acceptance of questionable doctrines, practices, and beliefs by calling them in terms other than what they are. Many such falsely labeled offerings are masquerading under the name of "truth," under the name of "liberty," of "freedom," "equality," and "reason." But the changing of the labels does not alter the contents of the package, and it is part of the responsibility of living for men to prove the contents of the things they choose to accept, and to look well beneath designing labels. In all the ways of life it is important to remember that poison is still deadly, even though the warning skull and bones has been removed.

❃ ❃ ❃

WE LIVE in an age of proving and disproving. The Lord God has set up standards for the conduct of men, and men have set up many standards for themselves. By methods of trial and error, by laboratory determination, and by countless other means, some less tangible than others, we are constantly determining what is truth and what is merely supposition. It is a wise thing for men to prove for themselves those things which can be proved without too great a sacrifice. But it is much greater wisdom to accept by the experience of the ages, and by the word of God, those things which cannot be proved except at too great a cost. It would undoubtedly be possible for every man to prove for himself that a life of sin and disobedience to law would lead to sorrow and regret. But for each man actually to prove this would be too costly. It would mean setting out upon a road on which there is no safety, and from which there is no sure return. And so, as a matter of wisdom and common sense, may we not accept as proof sufficient, by faith, by the testimony of wise men, by the experience of the generations, that some things are not good for man, and must therefore be left alone?

❋ ❋ ❋

THE thoughts of the world are merely the thoughts of men and women. The faith of the world and the deeds of the world are simply the faith and the deeds of men and women, even as you and I. And so the world can be no better than we are and no better than we think, because the world is merely you and I and our neighbors. And the world will never be better until you and I and our neighbors choose to make it better.

❋ ❋ ❋

ALL men have the God-given right to think and believe as they will, and all men have the God-given responsibility to render an accounting some-time, somewhere, for those things which they choose to think and to believe.

IV. Some Constants in a Changing World

"The lip of truth shall be established for ever: but a lying tongue is but for a moment."[53]

1. COMMENT ON TRUTH

So MANY good things have been tritely said that men are prone to think them commonplace and old-fashioned, failing to distinguish between the fundamental truth and the manner in which it is expressed. That is why the admonitions of parents sometimes become tiresome to children—because they are spoken over and over again in the same way and with the same pattern of words. It is unfortunate that thoughts should be burdened by words and that truth should be handicapped by our limited means of expressing it—but no matter how often we repeat a fundamental truth, and no matter how weary we may become of hearing it expressed and re-expressed, it is wisdom to remember that eternal verities are still eternal verities long after the words with which we give them expression have become threadbare. "Truth abideth and hath no end."[54]

❊ ❊ ❊

As LIFE moves on, it is well to be thoughtful in what we accept and what we reject. What millions acclaim is not necessarily worthy of acclaim. The surest indication that millions can be wrong is the fact that other millions are certain that they are wrong. What has stood the test of time is not necessarily worthy of endurance. An error a thousand years old is still an error. An untruth repeated a thousand times is still an untruth. And truth whether discovered today or known for centuries is absolute. 'And upon what would men build their lives if truth were a changing and a fickle thing?

Happily, truth is the same yesterday, today, and forever.

❋ ❋ ❋

IN A day of flagrant oratory and much speech-making, we are reminded that truth can usually be briefly stated but untruth often requires many words to cover the nature of its falsity. Perhaps that is why we so often find extended eloquence traveling hand in hand with questionable meanings. We are reminded of the Savior's comment, "They think that they shall be heard for their much speaking,"[55] and also of an older utterance: "A fool's voice is known by multitude of words."[56] The unadorned brevity of truth is always to be preferred to the ornamentation of a lie, no matter how attractive the latter may seem to be, or no matter at what price it is offered.

❋ ❋ ❋

THERE is a highly specialized modern art—and no doubt its origin is very ancient—which devotes itself to making things seem to be what they are not, to making facts seem to be something other than facts, and to making that which is something less than truth seem to be truth. This art has many forms and does its work under many names. Sometimes it is called propaganda, sometimes, more innocuously, publicity. Sometimes it is a political speech. It may be a misleading picture, an academic lecture, a religious dissertation, a document of statesmanship, or merely backdoor whispering, gossip, or innuendo—but whatever form it takes, its motive is always questionable, and its practice is always dangerous. It is the tool of demagogues, despots, and designing men. It is the enemy of

78

truth. Propaganda is that which uses or misuses fact for private motive, often with complete disregard for truth. Truth is that which dishonest men seek to refute or distort, and which honest men have no alternative but to accept. An ancient American prophet uttered a ringing cry which should be resounded down through the ages, in the heart of every man: "I glory in plainness; I glory in truth."[57]

❀ ❀ ❀

WHEN truth comes in conflict with a man's convenience, or with his traditional beliefs, there are several ways in which he may act toward it. He may pretend that he is not aware of its existence, thereby deceiving no one but himself. He may attempt to discredit it by assailing its verity. Or, perhaps at great cost, he may accept it for what it is and make it part of his life and philosophy. If he does, no matter what he pays for it, he has purchased wisely.

❀ ❀ ❀

CONCERNING the subject of truth much has been spoken and written; much has been argued and pondered. But of this we may be sure: What was fundamentally true when Adam walked with God, when David sang the psalms, when Solomon wrote his proverbs, when Shakespeare penned his plays, is still fundamentally true even today.

❀ ❀ ❀

NOT everything that is written is truth merely because we see it in print. Not everything that is spoken is truth merely because we hear it said. Not everything that is given picture portrayal is truth merely because it appears before our eyes. Not everything that is found in books is truth simply because it is enclosed between bound covers. Men write books, and men are not infallible.

❊ ❊ ❊

THROUGH the devious ways of life the seekers are the finders; the searchers are they who are rewarded by discovery; and, in the pursuit of all truth, all men approach nearer unto a knowledge and understanding of God. To them who seek earnestly and still have not found, there is yet hope. But to such as have ceased in their searchings, there is neither hope, nor comfort, nor promise of reward.

❊ ❊ ❊

PERHAPS one of the things we should keep uppermost in mind as we live from day to day is the fact that there is little to be gained by fighting anything that is incontrovertible. There is nothing to be gained by fighting against the laws of nature, but there is much to be gained by recognizing them and using them. There can be no possible benefit derived from fighting against truth, even though truth gives us inconvenience at times; but there is much to be reaped from accepting and working with the laws of truth. There is no good that can be accomplished by fighting against the purposes of God, even though, in our ignorance, we presume, at times, to disagree with them. But there is everything to be gained, both here and hereafter, by recognizing the purposes of God and patterning our lives in accordance with them, "for verily the voice of the Lord is unto all men, and there is none to escape; and there is no eye that shall not see, neither ear that shall not hear, neither heart that shall not be penetrated. . . . And the voice of warning shall be unto all people, . . . unto the day when the Lord shall come to recompense unto every man according to his work, and measure to every man according to the measure which he has measured to his fellow man."[58]

❀ ❀ ❀

WE MEN of earth seek refuge in many strange ways and from many things. Sometimes, like feudal lords of old, we wall up the approaches of our minds and close them to the onslaught of truth, only to find that all else crumbles before truth's eternal march.

❀ ❀ ❀

IN ALL the changing picture, it is good to keep in mind that while there is nothing so constant as change, neither is there anything so changeless as truth.

2. THE PRICE OF PRINCIPLE

HISTORY records that those men who have had courage to fight for ideals have often found much opposition and thankless rebuff, but time has honored their memories and brought peace to their souls. Some men who harbor ideals cloister them away and do not trouble a sometimes thoughtless world with their views. Others, without calculating personal losses, have tried to educate a world—a task which no one has yet quite been able to accomplish. Still others, with less strong conviction, have followed the easy way of compromise and have sacrificed ideals and principles here and there. If we can maintain our principles and ideals without being different, well and good. But if we cannot, the only thing in reason's name left for us to do is to be different. No matter how great the cost of living in accordance with what we know to be right, that cost is never so great as the price we pay for departing from it.

❋ ❋ ❋

To A generation softened by many conveniences and much pampering it is difficult to evaluate the thoughts, feelings, and experiences of our pioneer empire builders. We speak of their sacrifice; we hear of their deprivations; we read of their plodding journey, physical wants, frequent danger, and ceaseless toil. But our appreciation of them is more or less intellectual and remote. Their experiences are looked upon as stories of the past and are dismissed as belonging to another day. Perhaps we may never be called upon to endure like hardships.

82

Perhaps we shall. But whether we are or not it would be worth any price for this generation to learn this lesson from our pioneer fathers: It is always wisdom to exchange present convenience and comfort for future independence and integrity. It is never wise to forfeit principles now that will surely have to be redeemed at great cost in the future. Surely, if all of the pioneers of all times past could speak to this generation and to this nation, that would be the burden of their message. And would that we might say with them: "If God had commanded me to do all things I could do them."[59]

❀ ❀ ❀

THE kind of popularity that depends for its existence upon the sacrificing of ideals and principles never was and never will be worth the price that anyone ever paid for it. No one who sacrifices his own convictions for the superficial good opinion of others can ever hope to enjoy permanent respect or esteem. Much rather had we seek after acceptance among those people to whom the maintenance of a worthy ideal is a recommendation of the highest order.

❀ ❀ ❀

THROUGHOUT the generations of our history, men have fought and contended for many things. There have been times and places in which the struggle for mere physical sustenance was the paramount issue, but this is not so now—at least not in present-day America. In our day, he who is not gainfully employed may not starve, but the fact that physical sustenance may be had without effort, will not insure any man against moral, spiritual, and intellectual deterioration. In a machine age it is possible for a small part of the population to produce food, clothing, and shelter for all. But it is not possible for any man, in a machine age or in any other age, to give to others the moral, spiritual, and intellectual values that come with labor, service, and creative resourcefulness. No man transmits knowledge into experience except by doing. No man grows in spiritual or intellectual stature except by serving, creating, achieving. A generation that lives by the effort of others grows soft and strays from the principles and ideals that have built our heritage. We have never been more pressingly aware that the spirit and the body are the soul of man, and that both must be nourished. We cannot now, and never could, live by bread alone.

❊ ❊ ❊

IN THIS troubled but good world in which we live there is an endless conflict of forces, desires, attitudes, and beliefs. There is the force of good countered by the force of evil; the power of truth countered by the power of error; the desire of unorganized majorities held in abeyance by the rule of organized minorities. But through all the conflicts of which life is made up, there is no force so potent as the immovable, impenetrable force of a man who knows right from wrong and cleaves to the right without compromise; of a man who knows the rules of life and has lived by them; of a man who has faith in God, peace with his own conscience, and an unflinching place among his fellow men.

❊ ❊ ❊

SOME men uphold their ideals and cherish their convictions with admirable courage and unwavering loyalty. Others, who ofttimes theoretically believe in the same standards and principles, abandon

84

them on occasion for fear of being socially conspicuous—for fear of courting the disapproval of the unthinking crowd. But when such considerations cause us to waver, may it be remembered that to uphold an ideal is a social achievement of the highest order. The most enviable grace, the most admirable poise, the most lovable ease of manner, and the most engaging attractiveness belong to those who, with sincere dignity and tolerant conviction, are true to their ideals on all occasions.

❋ ❋ ❋

So LONG as we live in a world composed of people who do not accept a single law of conduct, a single standard of ethics, or a single code of morals, we shall have to face the problem of differences of opinion and disagreements among men. So long as we mingle socially and in business and in our schools and communities with people whose views and standards of living are not identical with ours, we shall be confronted with a choice between being different in some respects from other men, or sacrificing our own standards and beliefs for the sake of not being different.

❋ ❋ ❋

PERMIT us the use of a platitude—albeit a statement of irrevocable truth: "Virtue is its own reward." To none are these words so indelibly true as to those who have known them to be so by living a life of challenge to their verity. He who has a troubled conscience knows that virtue is its own reward. He who has been guilty of misconduct knows that principles and ideals are their own reason for being. He who has his wakeful hours embittered by remorse knows that the living of a good life needs no promise of reward hereafter, because such living bestows its rewards here and now.

❀ ❀ ❀

IN MATTERS of opinion, ofttimes it becomes a man to compromise, but in matters of truth and principle and moral right, they who travel the way of compromise find themselves upon a road which leads to worthless destinations and from which return is difficult. When conflicting views and confusing issues confront us, would that we could do our own thinking, and, using the eternal verities of God as our standard of measurement, would that our thinking could be right when we do it.

3. SINCERITY: GENUINE AND COUNTERFEIT

By way of excusing a man who has done the wrong thing there is sometimes offered in explanation the fact that he was sincere in what he was doing. While sincerity is usually listed among the virtues, we must keep in mind the possibility of being sincerely wrong. A man may be sincere in his persecution of other men, but the fact of his sincerity does not lessen the evils of persecution. Indeed, his very earnestness may enhance them. A man may be sincere in his intolerance and bigotry, and his sincerity may add vengeance to these other undesirable qualities. Men are usually sincere when they make bad investments, but the fact of their sincerity does not prevent their losing, ofttimes, the savings of a lifetime. And so it is imperative to remember that it is not only necessary for men to be sincere—it is necessary for them to be right. Faith in a wrong cause, work for an unworthy end, belief—even though sincere—in error and untruth, is a tragedy. Men must be more than sincere. They must be sincere—and right.

❊ ❊ ❊

We are aware that there is much counterfeiting going on in the world about us. Some of it the law takes note of and provides punishment for, but most of it is beyond the reach of any legal barrier or enforcement body. With varying degrees of success men counterfeit all manner of things. They pretend to be what they are not. They pretend an interest in people in whose welfare they have no interest

87

except as it can be useful to them. But of one thing we are most grateful and that is that a man cannot counterfeit sincerity with any sustained degree of success. He may be the world's most able actor. He may adopt the look, the manner, and the speech of a sincere man. He may practice the tone of voice, study the facial expression, and speak the words of those who are sincere, but there is an intangible something that enables the thoughtful and discerning to distinguish between a man who lives a life of sincerity and a man who only pretends to do so for the effect that it may have upon others. And for this we are led to express gratitude to that power which makes it so—that makes it possible to distinguish between the genuine and the counterfeit among those with whom we travel the ways of life.

❊ ❊ ❊

WE HERE pay our doubtful respects to a commodity which we have chosen to call social veneer. It is that manner of speech whereby people purport to put each other at ease, sometimes with sincere intent and sometimes with superficial condescension. It seems to smooth the surface waters of social situations, but does not alter or reveal the nature of the undercurrent. When sincerely applied, it is a virtue, as are all things that honestly smooth out human relationships. But when so thinly coated as to let the rough unloveliness of the real grain show through, it becomes a blighting vice. And may heaven protect us from those who, with feigned suavity, profess an interest in us and our welfare while being indifferent to it, or, even perchance, while secretly wishing for our discomfort or plotting our undoing.

❊ ❊ ❊

It is not superficiality of conduct that makes for greatness of character, but the motive which underlies that conduct. Most men are honest when it is to their advantage to be honest, but the test of character comes in being honest when to do so means personal loss and sacrifice. Many men will give freely of their means for a good cause when it seems to be the popular thing to do, but the test of generosity and brotherly kindness lies in giving when it is difficult to give or when there is no spotlight and no applause. Most men carry with them a veneer of courtesy and chivalry when the stage is set for such things, but the test of a gentleman and a virtuous man lies in his conduct in such matters when there is no gaze upon him. Neither the gloss of education, nor placement in the social register, nor a good publicity agent is proof of sterling qualities, nor able to erase the differences where there is lack of them. Greatness of character is determined only by that which a man and his God do not keep secret from each other. To this point of view the Savior of mankind paid His respects in the Sermon on the Mount when He suggested that men do and be what they are in secret and "thy Father which seeth in secret himself shall reward thee openly."[60]

❀ ❀ ❀

In a day when sensational and unrestrained publicity sometimes makes men seem to be what they are not—in a day when unchecked propaganda ignores truth and fact and sways the judgment of men, it is refreshing to recall the tersely stated words of the writer of Proverbs: "Remove far from me vanity and lies: . . . feed me with food convenient for me."[61] It is pleasant to think of that day when all things will be what they seem to be and when all men will seem to be what they are. Then shall we stand before God, unable to conceal our thoughts and desires with words and gestures that contradict the things that we are thinking and the motives that we are concealing. In the meantime we yearn for the time when the news that we hear and the things that we see and the rumors that confuse and contradict will be known and trusted quantities, in a world where seemingly no report may now be accepted at its face value.

❊ ❊ ❊

FOR the day in which we live may we suggest: Less regard for publicity and reputation, more regard for character; less regard for appearances, more regard for virtue; less haste in making promises, more speed in keeping them; less attention to popular approval, more regard for truth; less of sentimentality, more of true sentiment.

❊ ❊ ❊

IN OUR day we hear much about honesty. It has been variously defined and variously appraised. It seems that in the modern estimate of things there are degrees of honesty. Some men believe that honesty is a good thing—for all other men. Some men make it a part of their lives up to a certain point and beyond that—well, the pressure sometimes seems to be too great. Some men are honest in their business transactions, but lack honesty in their estimates of other men. Some men are honest outwardly, but are dishonest in their thoughts. Some men have one standard of honesty for the business day and another for the Sabbath. But in the eternal scheme of things, it is to be seriously doubted if there are degrees of honesty. From one way of thinking, a man is either honest or he is not. And such honesty is that quality which prevents a man even from deceiving himself in his innermost thoughts. It requires a superb kind of courage for a man to be sincerely honest with himself—but it brings with it superlative rewards of an inward peace and restfulness when we are.

❀ ❀ ❀

ORNATE language, devoid of sincerity, may for the moment, beget confusion in some, and may, for the moment, bring admiration from others. But simple language, burdened with a message of plain and honest truth, strikes deep into the hearts and thoughts of men when first it is spoken, and resounds with its ageless ringing down through the avenues of time.

❀ ❀ ❀

WHEN so many claims are being made for so many things, and at a time when so many convincing misstatements are rampant, it reminds one of the responsibility of each, to be sure that his thinking is right. A man who is sincerely deceived is one thing, but a man who is sincerely right is, obviously, another—and the two do not find themselves in the same pastures, either here or hereafter.

4. *THE QUALITY OF SUCCESS*

THERE is an all too prevalent disposition, as there always has been wherever there has been human nature, to state success in terms of material acquisition or public acclaim. It is as though success had become a synonym for wealth or position; as though to say that a man is successful is to say that he has gathered around him many material possessions and has invited himself to the attention of many people. But these things may or may not have anything to do with success. Whether or not a man is successful depends upon whether or not he has attained his objective. If one man sets out for the east and another for the west and each reaches his intended destination, each is successful in his venture, despite the fact that their separate ways have led them to places far removed. If a man's intended purpose in life is to rear a useful and respected family, to make a plant to grow where none has grown before, to render a service where no service has been given, to build a home where none has been before, in the doing of these things he finds success no matter what his financial rating or his publicity value. In one sense, a man may be successful in an errand of evil, if he sets out upon an unworthy purpose and accomplishes it—but in an absolute sense there is no success except for those who travel the course that leads toward those eternal values among which are numbered peace, happiness, the honest respect of men, the approbation of God, and a sense of having lived life well—and neither publicity nor fame nor financial increment has anything to do with these things.

❋ ❋ ❋

THAT which they have is not nearly so important to men as that which they do. Pride of possession is never so great as joy of achievement. The labor that is in the doing is more to be cherished than work that is already finished. When there is no more work to be done, the reason for living and the desire to live will have vanished—but that time will never come.

❋ ❋ ❋

FEW men there are but who have unfulfilled longings. Few there are but who have striven for something unattained. This righteous discontent, this rational unrest, is the secret of the never-ending progress of mankind. If there were limits to longing there would be limits to moving. If there were limits to worthy desire, there would be limits to progress. But, thanks be to God, there are no such limits to halt the eternal quest.

❋ ❋ ❋

ONE of the most universal wishes of humanity is that humanity were somehow different. Even those we love sincerely, we love with an awareness of their faults. We yearn always for better things in men. We cherish and respect our neighbors and friends but wish that we did not see in them those traits of human weakness which are common in greater or less degree to all mortal men, and with which we, ourselves, are so generously endowed, and to which we are blind, or partially so, in our own lives. In short, we wish that other men were different; but since they are as they are, we must accept them as they are and help them to become better than they are. Any movement, creed, or society that does less than this, does not justify its own existence. The Lord Himself, when He walked the earth, did not expect perfection in men. He chose unlettered fish-

93

ermen to be His apostles, and helped them to broader vision and greater service. The primary purpose of all human endeavor is to take men as they are and help them to become better. And on that day when we lose sight of this reason for our existence, we shall be without a purpose worthy of perpetuation. In the wisdom of Providence, finding ourselves as we are, it is our eternal hope that we shall continually become better than we are, and, the Lord being willing, we shall so move on together.

❊ ❊ ❊

THAT which is required of men has been summarized by the brief and oft-repeated sentence "Unto whomsoever much is given, of him shall be much required."[62] To repeat this axiom in other language: Our obligations will be commensurate with our opportunities; our reward will be proportionate to our service; our condemnation will be in accordance with our neglect. Living in an age and in a land blessed above all others, which we do, means that no trivial or ordinary service from us will be acceptable to the Great Judge of all things.

❊ ❊ ❊

ACCORDING to the record of myth, legend, and history, the men of this earth have placed their trust in a great variety of things as the relentless passing of the years has found the human drama enacting itself over and over again. The strong arm, the smooth tongue, the magic power of money, and the strategy of good logic based on false premise are a few among the false gods in which misguided men have relied for strength, sustenance, and support. Momentarily, perhaps a measure of success has seemed to follow, but the things that these men

94

have worked for they could not take with them when they departed hence, nor could they insure a perpetuation of them after they left for another scene of activity. And the long look back tells us, as surely as we have the courage to turn and view it, that the only men who could ever face the end of life's journey with an abiding inward peace and an unshakable assurance of greater things yet to come, were those men who could say with the prophet of old: In Thee, O Lord, have I trusted.

❃ ❃ ❃

WE HEAR much about success. Success in life is clearly a relative term. Whether or not a man feels he is successful depends upon his standards and the standards of his friends by which he is accustomed to measure his achievements. But of this we may be sure: whatever degree of success is attained by anyone, that success is attributable to living and doing consistently. Sudden bursts of endeavor, occasional acts of charity, short-lived flights of industry, and brief interludes of circumspect living lead no man to any measurable degree of success.

5. "BE STILL, AND KNOW THAT I AM GOD"

IT WAS spoken and written anciently in the code of conduct given to men of God: "Thou shalt not take the name of the Lord thy God in vain; for the Lord will not hold him guiltless that taketh his name in vain."[63] In the thoughtless speech of men there is an all too prevalent and careless use of the name of Deity. Would it not seem that if a man believed in God and feared Him, he would also fear to defile the name of God by letting it pass thoughtlessly from his lips? Would it not seem also that if a man believed not in God, his oath were then meaningless, and his speaking of the name of Deity were lacking in point, and would better have been unspoken?

❀ ❀ ❀

BY THE recorded words of the prophets, there have been described those conditions which seem to have their counterpart in the world we see about us: "And there shall be upon the earth distress of nations, with perplexities; the sea and the waves roaring, and in that day shall be heard of wars and rumors of wars, and the whole earth shall be in commotion, and men's hearts shall fail them. And the love of men shall wax cold, and iniquity shall abound, for fear shall come upon all people."[64] But fortunately, above all the vain clamor, muddled thinking, and short-sighted motives, we seem to hear a voice that says now, as it always has and always will: "Be still, and know that I am God."[65]

❀ ❀ ❀

To ONE who loved the Lord and His ways, but found times when his faith was not sufficient to follow in all things, it was spoken thus: "And behold, how oft you have transgressed the commandments and the laws of God, and have gone on in the persuasions of men . . . You should not have feared man more than God. Although men set at naught the counsels of God, and despise his words, yet you should have been faithful; and he would have extended his arm and supported you against all the fiery darts of the adversary; and he would have been with you in every time of trouble . . . fear not what man can do, for God shall be with you forever and ever."[66]

❁ ❁ ❁

LOOKING back upon the record of scripture and of history it becomes apparent that men of the past, even as many of our own day, have followed after false gods, or have supposed that there is no God, and have gloried in their own strength. Time and the immutable laws of living have taken care of all such in the past—but our own generation we would persuade against such folly. Even as the Lord said upon Sinai: "Thou shalt have no other gods before me," so is the same voice and the same commandment unto this day and this people. And each age has found the cure for its plagues when men could say, with the ancients of Israel: "Thou, even thou, art Lord alone."[67]

❁ ❁ ❁

BEFORE men remove from their lives an unalterable belief in the literal reality of a living God, they should make sure that they have something adequate to fill the void that abandonment of such belief will surely leave. Whom else can we ap-

97

proach in prayer? Who else can control the forces of nature? From what other source can we look for new life? Where else may we seek comfort when death comes, as it does to all men? There is no void so great, no loneliness so complete, as that of a man who thinks he has removed God from his life and who finds that he has nothing with which to replace the truth and reality which he imagines he has rejected. "By these things we know that there is a God in heaven, who is infinite and eternal, from everlasting to everlasting the same unchangeable God, the framer of heaven and earth, and all things which are in them; and that he created man, male and female, after his own image and in his own likeness, created he them."[68]

❀ ❀ ❀

"If a man say, I love God, and hateth his brother, he is a liar: for he that loveth not his brother whom he hath seen, how can he love God whom he hath not seen?"[69]

V. From the Record of Time and Experience

"God . . . will render to every man according to his deeds."[70]

1. *POVERTY AND PLENTY*

CONCERNING the rich and the poor, the prophets have spoken eloquently, and occasionally it is challenging and revealing to recall their words on this subject of persistent perplexity: "Wo unto you rich men, that will not give your substance to the poor, for your riches will canker your souls; and this shall be your lamentation in the day of visitation, and of judgment, and of indignation: The harvest is past, the summer is ended, and my soul is not saved!" So much for the rich. And of the poor it is said: "Wo unto you poor men, whose hearts are not broken, whose spirits are not contrite, . . . and whose hands are not stayed from laying hold upon other men's goods, whose eyes are full of greediness, and who will not labor with your own hands!"[71]

❀ ❀ ❀

WE ARE expressing no new thought when we remind ourselves that there is as much work in the world to be done today as there ever was. There are as many unsatisfied wants—as many unfulfilled needs—and that which is as yet undiscovered is illimitable. If there be those for whom gainful employment cannot be found, it is not because there is no work to be done—but because there is some breakdown somewhere along the line of human relationships. There is dire need for men who will accept a trust and keep it—for men in whom are found intelligence and integrity—for men who know that they must serve one master with loyalty, and remember what belongs to them and what belongs to another—for men who know that a day's work must be given for a day's wage, and that the world owes them nothing except as they earn it, even as the Lord God said they should when he cast their first parents out of the Garden of Eden.

❋ ❋ ❋

SHOULD there come a day when men become too modern to keep the commandments of the Lord, too modern to repent and return to ways of righteousness, in that day also men will have become too modern to enjoy peace, or to find it, and too modern to be prospered of the Lord. From the word of scripture comes this rule of life, tersely stated and eternally true: "Inasmuch as ye shall keep my commandments, ye shall prosper in the land. And again it is said that: Inasmuch as ye will not keep my commandments ye shall be cut off from the presence of the Lord."[72]

❋ ❋ ❋

THE cycle of the ages reveals that pride and prosperity are followed by poverty and humility. It would be well if a people could prosper and remember the laws of righteousness. But if we must have prosperity and forgetfulness, or adversity and humble remembrance, the latter were much the more to be desired.

❋ ❋ ❋

HE WHO wrote the Psalms left us these words which have power to bring peace to troubled hearts: "Fret not thyself because of evil-doers, neither be thou envious against the workers of iniquity. For they shall soon be cut down like the grass, and wither as the green herb. Trust in the Lord, and do good; so shalt thou dwell in the land, and verily thou shalt be fed. . . . A little that a righteous man hath is better than the riches of many wicked."[73]

* * *

THEY who live in poverty seek plenty. They who have plenty seek peace, security, and happiness. Always there is discontent. Always there is unrest. The fulfillment of each desire gives rise to other desires yet unfulfilled. And so it will be until regard for things spiritual will have overtaken the regard for things material and until the conquest of self will have equalled the conquest of environment.

* * *

As WE look about us we are impressed with the fact that men pay a price for each of their possessions. He who has nothing, has nothing to lose, nothing to defend, nothing to live up to, and he lives in danger of becoming a member of that irresponsible group which carries its loyalties on the gust of a wind and changes them as often as the wind changes. He who is moderately well established becomes a pillar of society. He has a home to defend against the inroads of false beliefs and disintegrating practices. He stands with his back to his hearthstone and makes it difficult for the world to go far wrong in either direction. But he who has acquired possessions beyond all the reasonable needs of himself and his family, is always in the position of protecting and defending that which he can neither fully use nor completely enjoy. He may be a shameless prodigal, but more likely he is a great benefactor of mankind; he may use his wealth for wasteful and selfish purposes, but more likely he builds great industries, gives employment to thousands, and endows noble enterprises. But regardless of his worthiness or unworthiness, he is always the target of

103

those who would part him from his money and of those who, failing this purpose, impute unto him all manner of evil designs and unholy practices— because covetous eyes are always roving and covetous hands are always reaching for another man's goods—in public places, in private life, and in the substrata of society. We pay a price for all of our possessions. Some are worth any price, but for some we pay too much.

❀ ❀ ❀

"And in my prosperity I said, I shall never be moved."[74]

2. PERENNIAL EQUATION: YOUTH AND AGE

THE equation of youth and age still plays its part, as it always has in the past. To youth looking forward, life seems abundantly long for limitless achievement. To age looking back, the life we know seems all too short for the realization of things hoped for, for the accomplishment of things desired. And that is why the wisdom of age may rightfully counsel the ambition of youth. No one knows better than they who are nearing the end of the journey how precious are the moments that pass; how utterly lost are the wasted hours; how relentlessly beyond recall are those things which we sometimes do, which, being looked back upon, are a source of regret.

❀ ❀ ❀

THE relentless passing of the seasons finds men quickly growing older. While age holds no remorse for those who have lived their lives in season, many of the disappointed men we see around us are they who have lived unseasonable lives. They have let spring pass by without using the season for its intended purpose, and then, realizing too late the error of neglect, they have tried to do spring's work in summer, and summer's work in autumn, and winter has found them with no harvest. By youth, may it be remembered that there are none so hopelessly handicapped as they who have let pass by the time for preparation, and who go forth to live their lives out of season.

❀ ❀ ❀

WE HAVE long glibly quoted: "The hand that rocks the cradle, rules the world." So often have we said it that we have ceased to question whether or not it be true. In a modern world the hand that rocks the cradle sometimes does not rock it very long. From the moment a child begins to toddle in the neighborhood his outlook on life is partly determined by his home and partly by others. At a very tender age a goodly part of his waking hours is taken over by a school whose policies and influences and teachings and attitudes and methods are determined by sources quite remote from the home. By our modern impersonal way of doing things, his social environment is quite likely to be largely colored by commercial interest and profit motive, and the other elements of community life are also likely to have a sort of steam-roller aspect, powered by forces far removed from "the hand that rocks the cradle." A kind of super-machine that we have created or have permitted to be created rules the cradle and the hand that rocks it and the child that comes from it. By all of those influences and teachings and practices that make up our impersonal social, civic, and educational background, responsibility seems to have become a thing once removed from us. But it cannot long remain so, and, fundamentally, it never could be so. We have never really transferred our obligations in the matter of teaching our children, or in any other matter, even though we may have talked ourselves into thinking we have. To quote the record of scripture: "And again, inasmuch as parents have children . . . that teach them not to understand . . . the sin be upon the heads of the parents. . . . And they shall also teach their children to pray, and to walk uprightly before the Lord."[75] So much for the duty of parents. And may it also be added that the obligation of those who teach the children of others is one of solemn sacredness, and any servant of society who teaches for truth anything more or less than truth, stands self-condemned before the Highest Tribunal.

❈ ❈ ❈

MAY we say a word to youth? In every life there comes an awakening, and with it the fading of many dreams. There comes a day when we realize that the world is no longer waiting for us to prepare for life. It is waiting for us to live it—to face its realities, to solve its problems, to improve its conditions, and to do for the next generation what has been done for us. So comes the awakening that forces us to face realities, and most happy is he who faces them with full purpose. The job is not easy! Who but a weakling would wish that it were? The problems have not all been solved! Who but a dullard would want them to be? The future is unpredictable! Read your histories! When wasn't it? The world is so greatly changing! Be thankful for that, so long as principles and ideals and ultimate destination do not change. And so we envy rather than pity youth, for theirs is the future and all that belongs thereto.

❈ ❈ ❈

To THIS age and civilization it may be said: Your schools are doing much toward giving our youth a rich store of classified knowledge and methodical habits of thinking. Your churches are doing much toward maintaining religious traditions and preserving a consciousness of reverence and the fundamental virtues. Your other social institutions are all helping in their way to keep the world livable. But you moderns—with all your creative ingenuity—have never brought forth a substitute for a good home or a virtuous mother. So long as children are taught truth and honor and reverence by the family fireside, this world we know and love, despite its weaknesses, is safe. But take from us the integrity of home and none there is who would care to say toward what end our ways would lead.

* * *

IN THE world we see about us—and perhaps it has always been so—there is a disposition when we give, to give carelessly, in the most expedient manner but not necessarily in the best way. There are some things we can give our children without any effort on their part—but the most precious things of life we cannot give them unless they be willing to pay the price of possession. With little or no effort we can accept from another or give to another the tangible things of earth—money, food, and all manner of commodities, but they who suppose that material heritage may be seized and enjoyed without effort are steeped in their own folly, because the greatest rewards of living come with growth of mind and enlargement of spirit, and a man shrivels within himself if these he does not have. If we could learn to give to the end that our children would grow from within, the outward things of life would take care of themselves. But if we bestow upon others material bounties without an inward preparedness, we shall dwarf their souls with the stunting influence of our own misguided generosity and careless giving.

* * *

MAY we speak of one of those things for which all the thankfulness we have is yet not adequate— thankfulness that our fathers kept faith with us and counted no sacrifice too great to bequeath their children a right to freedom in a free land. There were many things they could not achieve in their day, but they did not destroy the future by any unwillingness to meet and to solve and to pay for their own problems and perplexities. We have learned one of the greatest lessons of life when we learn to live not only for ourselves but also for those who follow. Some of the greatest satisfactions men ever achieve, come not directly to them, but to their children. Those things which we would have liked for ourselves and which we have reached for but fallen short of, we often realize with greater joy by making it possible for our children to achieve them. And a man has never known one of the greatest compensations in life until he has had the surpassing vicarious experience of seeing himself and his plans projected into the next generation. That is how the race was builded. That is how civilization has grown—by the debt each generation pays to those who follow, since they cannot pay their debt otherwise to those who have gone before. And so we are grateful that our fathers kept faith with us, and we ask for strength and wisdom of foresight to pass on to our children and our children's children a free and unfettered heritage, unburdened by any compromising ways of ours.

❋ ❋ ❋

IN A day when there is confusion in the hearts of many, it is of youth that we are particularly concerned; and for them, and for all others whom it may please to accept it, we offer a guide for conduct: If life is not what it ought to be, it is yours to make it what it should be. Change whatever you wish to change, within the limits of truth, noble ideals, and fundamental principles, and your generation, and generations yet unborn, will call you blessed. But remember also that there are steadfastly in the heavens those things which change not and are eternal. Be solemnly sure that you cast not from out of your lives any of them, for nothing will ever be found to take their place.

❊ ❊ ❊

FUNDAMENTALLY, there need be no conflict between the ambition of youth and the caution of age. To youth has been given the driving force that moves the world forward despite discouraging obstacles. To age has been given the tempering wisdom that directs the energy of youth in tried and proved channels. Sacred history records that the Lord has selected his strong men from the ranks both of youth and of age. The world has need of both, and each has need of the other.

❊ ❊ ❊

IF THERE have been misdeeds in our youth, it is well to repent of them and to depart from them in our age. If there have been departings from the ways of righteousness in age, it is well to be able to look back upon a more circumspect time of living in our youth. But in the picture of the eternal progress of man, there is no time more opportune than any other for taking misdirected steps or living in unholy ways. Youth is as much a part of eternity as age. Age is as much a part of the endless picture as youth. And so it is well for us, in age and youth alike, to see that nothing enters the conduct of our lives that will blemish the picture as we look back upon it a decade or a century or an age from now. Pleasant memories are the welcome companions of our aging years. Things that are later worthy to become pleasant memories should be the garnered treasure of youth. "Learn wisdom in thy youth; yea, learn in thy youth to keep the commandments of God . . . Let the affections of thy heart be placed upon the Lord forever."[76]

THAT which men plan to do they should begin early and pursue diligently. Many who might have become great benefactors to humanity have delayed too long the pursuit of the thing for which they were best fitted and have passed into age and obscurity, never having risen above things mediocre. Many who have intended well have passed through their best years always intending, but never doing. It is true that eternity lies ahead, but it is also true that today we must take at least one step in the desired direction if we are to move toward greater achievement.

3. LEADERS AND LEADERSHIP

IN PONDERING the present course of the world, the matter of leadership seems to demand some comment, since it is apparent that great and worthy peoples may easily be misled, to their own sorrow, and to the sorrow of many others. Assuming responsibility for the direction and leadership of others is a task of grave proportions, even for the strongest and best informed men. Acting for oneself and advising others how to act are things vastly different. They who have assumed leadership, whether in matters social, political, moral or religious, should prayerfully consider the course to which they direct others, lest they be held accountable for having been false leaders.

❊ ❊ ❊

NEITHER history nor the experience of our daily living justifies the conclusion that any man, no matter how important or useful he may be, is indispensable to the welfare of the world or to the progress of the society in which he lives. Statesmen, soldiers, writers, artists, men of religion, of science, and of finance—all take the long journey and travel beyond the ken of mortality in the Lord's own due time; and, thanks be to Providence, to each generation and age, and to each country and people, is given its leaders that men may follow and that the world may move on, regardless of the coming and going of favored sons and brilliant intellects. God so wills and orders it, as the story of the centuries testifies.

❊ ❊ ❊

THOSE men who rise to inspired heights and who leave the world permanently enriched for all who come thereafter have found themselves somehow in touch with the source of all truth and wisdom and have beheld such broadening horizons that no room was left in their lives for the usual fears and enslaving shackles that hold so many of us down below the range of wide and open vision.

❀ ❀ ❀

LIFE deals out its reverses much too indiscriminately for any of us to presume that we have attained a station above its humbling influences. A nameless lad today may rule an empire tomorrow. A prince today may shortly be a pauper. The Creator of men is no respecter of persons and His gifts of intelligence, leadership, and creative genius are showered among the children of the obscure as well as among those of high station.

❀ ❀ ❀

CALMNESS and tranquillity and assurance in life are acquired by conscious effort and not by accidental bestowal. As we go about the earnest business of living from day to day, there are influences at work in the lives of all of us that would destroy our faith, shatter our reason, and rob us of our peace if we would but let them. Our strong men and our leaders are not such as have never been troubled with such influences. Rather, they have faced and conquered those forces which would unbalance and take from us the calm richness of living.

❀ ❀ ❀

IN LIGHT of the current disposition to give artificial support to every conceivable manner of thing, we are prompted to ask ourselves what makes for greatness in men—what has gone into the making of those who have risen to serve their generations. To answer the query specifically would mean to recount the individual biography of each, but in general we may say without a tenable, dissenting vote that men are great not because they have been spared the hardships of life but because they have overcome them—because Providence has given them courage, not protection; faith, not a favored lot; integrity, not freedom from temptation. Greatness has not come easily to any man. Nor is greatness ever bestowed without price. God so rules that the eternal principle of self-effort must be dominant even in a day of pampering, if life is to be worth while to them who cherish it and all its problems.

* * *

As WE see about us the flagrant misuse of those forces and materials which our modern civilization has brought into being, we are impressed with the great need for faith among men and regard for the spiritual considerations of life. The man of cold and calculating intellect, largely devoid of faith, ofttimes makes a great factual discovery, but he is usually not impressed with its moral implications. He does not see his discovery in relation to the purpose of life and the ultimate destination of men. He may perfect an automobile, but he does not tell us whether to use it for saving or destroying life. He may find a new drug, but he does not tell us whether to use it for human good or for human wreckage. But it is not enough to discover a fact or perfect a machine. All things must be interpreted and evaluated and used in terms of human progress and happiness here and hereafter, and it is only the man of faith who can do this—who can convert the findings of scholarship and research into ways of morality, and give eternal meaning to all of the facts of the universe that are or may yet be discovered.

❀ ❀ ❀

A PROPHET, facing the prospect of an early death, left these words for us to ponder: "If my life is of no value to my friends, it is of no value to myself."[77] By this rule a man may judge the usefulness of his life and leadership. No man who lives unto himself, and for himself, to the exclusion of all others, has much that is worth preserving, according to the generally accepted rules of life. If my life is of no value to my friends, it is of no value to me. And by all standards of living, both for things here and things hereafter, he who serves best his own generation receives unto himself the greatest rewards that life can give.

❀ ❀ ❀

THERE are many qualifications of leadership, but none more important than reverence, love of truth, and prayerfulness. It is as difficult to imagine the great men who have built America lacking in these, as it would be false. Those men whom we remember with honor are men whom we can picture with bowed and uncovered heads, seeking help and wisdom from the Giver of all good things. Our most cherished picture of Washington is not that of a triumphant general, but that of a man kneeling in prayer at Valley Forge. Of Lincoln we remember dark days of sorrow when the divine source of comfort and help was repeatedly and constantly sought. Of the Master, even Jesus Christ, we remember Gethsemane and the prayer upon the cross.

OUT of the days of our living, we learn to know that there are limits within which we can order our lives, and limits beyond which we cannot order them. We learn that each day brings something to be faced, whether it be unto happiness or unto sorrow. We learn that peace does not mean that there shall be no more struggle, and we learn in the hour of despair that time and the goodness of God have a way of easing all burdens and healing all wounds. We learn that after we have done our utmost in accordance with the wisdom and circumstances that have been given unto us, we must meet life as it comes; and we save ourselves much bitterness and remorse when we learn to say with that faith which the Lord God has made possible to all His children: Thy will, O Lord, not mine be done.

❈ ❈ ❈

ONE of the seemingly unfortunate circumstances of life is the manner in which the innocent are called upon to suffer with the guilty. If misfortune came only to those who were responsible for it, we would welcome it as an avenging angel, but, in the complexity of our living, trouble visits whom it will, and when it is started in one place it travels to another. Dishonesty in high places causes misery all down the line. The failure of a financial institution, the misuse of public funds, the inroads of a racketeer, the wild careening of a drunken driver, or the perpetration of a war, spread hurt and sorrow and human suffering far beyond the province of those who are directly responsible. We would ofttimes be led to think upon the unfairness of life except for our unshakable faith in the unfailing wisdom and justice of God our Father. Neither here nor hereafter shall we ever find any innocent victim of an evil, who would be willing to change places with the man by whom the evil was set upon its way. To carry a conscience of guilt around in this life is punishment enough through all the sleeping and waking hours of those who have it. And then, after that, add unto this present punishment those things that shall transpire before the judgment bar of God—and we have ample justice by way of penalties for the guilty and sure compensation for those who suffer unjustly by the hands of others.

❋ ❋ ❋

PERHAPS the most anguished words of all scripture are those of Jesus when He was upon the cross and cried with a loud voice, saying: "My God, my God, why hast thou forsaken me?"[78] Many a man in his hour of need and despair has felt even as this, and has wondered what he has done to deserve the lot wherewith he finds himself and has wondered where indeed is that God and Father of all who marks the fall of the sparrow and looks over all creatures with love and justice and mercy. To all who have at one time or another found themselves thinking such thoughts, perhaps it should be said that man sees things only as they are and knows neither the beginning nor the end. Even as the motives of a parent may be misunderstood by the mind of a child, so does the wisdom of God transcend the thinking of man. He, our Creator, sees not only what is, but what has gone before and what shall follow. Having set our minds to an attitude of such trust, we find ourselves living in peace,

117

with fortitude to endure all things even unto the end.

❉ ❉ ❉

THERE are two manner of experiences that enter into the life of every man: those which we plan for ourselves and those which come in spite of all our planning. Sometimes, happily, we fare better than we had honestly hoped, and sometimes, unhappily, we fall far short of achieving those things for which we have striven. No matter how well we seem to control the elements which affect our lives, there are always to be considered things unlooked for. Surely it must be better that way. It would be difficult to imagine a more unsatisfactory existence than the life of a man into which nothing unexpected ever came. Furthermore, it is all part of a great plan. The Lord still chasteneth whom He loveth and all those things which come into our lives in spite of our best laid plans are part of the education and enriching experience of every child of God who walks the earth. We may think what we would like for ourselves and then, in the spirit of that resignation born of faith, we must reconcile ourselves at one time or another to accept what life presents.

❉ ❉ ❉

EVEN if there were a means of cloistering oneself away to avoid facing the realities of life, it is doubtful if many of us would do so. Too much shelter is as little to be desired as too little shelter. He who has not lived a life that presents a many-sided picture, has missed much, and the loss is all the more bitter for his knowing naught of it. He who has not lived above sorrow, who has not faced fear with courage, who has not faced work with a zest for its

118

doing, and difficulty with a thrill for its over-coming, has precious much yet to live and learn.

* * *

MEN desire ease, seek comfort, and yearn for tranquillity, but the monotony of an untroubled existence is as quickly to be tired of as the burden of unbroken adversity. Life must be varied to be endured, and when we pray for surcease from all of life's problems, we pray for that which we would probably not enjoy, even though it were granted.

* * *

THERE is no adversity in life that may not have its triumph; there are none so ill done by but that they may not have hearts full of thanksgiving. And despite all our troubles, life must still go on, today and tomorrow and during all time to come. When it seems oppressively difficult, it may be comforting to remember that countless others have faced all manner of heartaches and disappointments and have walked serenely confident to that end which is not an end but a beginning. And at such times it is good to remember also that adversity comes ever to an end, even as all other mortal experiences must have an ending.

* * *

THAT men grow and that the world progresses by adversity is neither an idle axiom nor a thoughtless saying. Rising above life's many disappointments is a sure mark of greatness in men. With hopes shattered, with cherished desires frustrated, with labors brought to naught, there are those in the world who, because of their unwavering faith in the ultimate triumph of all good, rise from the trials of living as surely as the sun rises at the dawning of each day. It is such courageous men who sorrow not that the task is great, but rejoice that their strength is equal to the thing that they must do.

❋ ❋ ❋

WE HAVE heard of many high-sounding philosophies of life, beautiful in theory, lovely to think upon. But what each man should ask concerning his own philosophy is this: What does it do for me? If you can see hopes and ambitions and years of effort shattered, and charge it off to experience and begin again at whatever age—if you can see injustice and corruption and the inhumanity of man to man, and not curse God, but lay the blame where it belongs, at the door of man's disobedience, wilfulness, and greed—if you can see death lay its hand upon the brow of one beloved and find no bitterness in your heart, but fill the void with a certain knowledge that as there has now been a parting there will yet be another meeting where friend will never part with friend—if you can refrain from placing undue emphasis upon the tangibles of life and bring yourself to realize that as you came forth naked so will you return, taking nothing of your labor except enriched experience, increased intelligence, and the blessing of the goodness you have brought your fellow man—if you can do these things, really do them, then your philosophy of life is something to be cherished. Keep it until something surely better comes along to take its place. But if these things you cannot do, seek until you find a way—for such an outlook upon life is worth whatever price is asked for it.

❋ ❋ ❋

OF THE uncounted millions who have lived and died, and of the great hosts of men and women who dwell on earth today, it may be safely said that no one ever passed through the experience of life without knowing trouble, anguish, and misfortune, in one form or another. Unwavering faith may or may not protect us from some of life's adversities. Merely earnestly wishing for something or earnestly praying for something does not always assure it unto us. With our limited foresight we often discern vaguely if at all what is for our best good, and some things come to us despite our faith and earnest supplication, for the enrichment of the experience of life. And so, when we have earnestly asked for what we think we want, we must leave the issue to a Higher Wisdom than ours.

❊ ❊ ❊

MANY of us are guilty of letting our lives become lost in a daily routine. We build habits of thought and action and suppose ourselves to be secure in them. We rather imagine that our established procedure is of considerable importance to us and to the world in which we move, and as long as life proceeds smoothly, we do not really know the relative value of the things about us, nor do we know how well prepared we are to meet the shocks and stresses and sorrows that at one time or another come to all of us. But let someone cherished pass from us, or an illness lay us low, or a calamity take from us our material security and accustomed habits of living, and we see life stripped to its bare essentials. What we have left is not what we had supposed was important at all. We know then that the important things are not our material possessions nor our daily routine nor our precious comfort; rather life becomes a matter of permanent values—friends, loved ones, exalted thoughts, work to do, and a calm assurance of the eternal permanency of

121

the human soul, and an unquestioning belief in the wisdom and goodness of our Eternal Father. Blessed is the man who can put his feet on such foundations and not be shaken by the storms of life. And those who cannot face the buffetings with such well-grounded assurance are in danger of becoming cynical with confusion and sorrow in their hearts.

5. PEACE: WITHIN AND WITHOUT

NOT all conflict is on the field of battle. Not all warring is between peoples and nations. The turmoils that may rage in a human heart when desire struggles with conscience, when service opposes selfishness, and when immediate pleasure counters the prospect of limitless achievement is the conflict that destroys the peace of men even when armed forces wage no war. He who has mastered self has found peace, even though there be no peace around him.

❋ ❋ ❋

BECAUSE the world has not found peace there be those of cynical mind and those of discouraged heart who say that Christianity has failed, that religion has failed, that idealism has failed, and even that God has failed. And to all such let it be said that if a man dies because he refuses to do what his physician prescribes it does not prove that the physician was wrong. Long ago the Great Physician prescribed for all of the ills of the world. And because we have taken the prescription only lightly if at all, it appears that we shall have to take the consequences in other and more drastic ways. "Thou shalt have no other gods before me—Thou shalt not take the name of the Lord thy God in vain—Remember the Sabbath day to keep it holy—Six days shalt thou labor—Honor thy father and thy mother —Thou shalt not kill—Thou shalt not commit adultery—Thou shalt not steal—Thou shalt not bear false witness—Thou shalt not covet—Thou shalt love thy neighbor as thyself"—these things have not failed, but men have failed to give them place in their lives, and for this failure of ours—not of God's nor of His principles—are we to substitute the might of arms, machines of destruction, the intrigue of statesmen, the promises of despots, the rule of force, the slaying of men, the banishment of freedom, and the death of security! May God help us and all men our brethren to believe and observe those principles which have always brought peace and happiness, before we are brought low by those forces which have always dealt misery and destruction.

❋ ❋ ❋

THESE things are the spoilers of our inward peace: The fear that lies in the human heart and reminds us of our weakness; the memory of things that should never have been done; the confusion that lurks in the human mind when the line of demarcation between truth and error is obscured; the consciousness of time's passing quickly by without our having freighted it with a full measure of achievement; deference to idle opinions, though they be in discord with age-old statements of eternal truth; vanity and love of self, which sometimes lead us to think and act lower than human intelligence would justify.

❋ ❋ ❋

EXCEPT life itself, there is probably nothing that men cherish as much as peace. And perhaps more of us do not find it because we do not understand the nature of peace. Men and nations alike run to and fro in search of it, some hoping to purchase it at a bargain, some fully expecting to pay its entire price, but not knowing what price must be paid. Perhaps they have forgotten, perhaps they never knew, that peace does not depend upon the substance of material things, nor upon the accident of chancing to be in one place or another, but rather peace belongs to an attitude of mind which leaves the windows of the soul open to all truth and the will to live in accordance with that truth. And this they should know who think that peace may be found by restless journeying from one place to another.

❈ ❈ ❈

NEITHER the memory of man nor the history of the ages can recall when any great difference of opinion was settled permanently by force, when anyone was convinced by coercion, or when humanity was uplifted by warfare. A peace-loving people will fight when forced to defend its rights and liberties, but the treasured and worth-while memories of our lives are the memories of peace and not the memories of strife.

❈ ❈ ❈

"IF THOU hadst known . . . in this thy day, the things which belong unto thy peace! but now they are hid from thine eyes."[79] And since these words were uttered, and through long ages before, thoughtful men have asked: What are the things which belong unto our peace? Perhaps this question could best be answered by asking another: What are the things which destroy our peace? The answer is plain to thoughtful men—greed, unholy ambitions, crooked thinking. In short, those things which destroy our peace are the things which at all times and in all ages have been forbidden to men by the Lord God and the wisdom of experience. We know that law is law, and we know that the same causes produce the same effects, as they always have and always will, both in human behavior and in the physical world. And we know, therefore, that the price of peace is obedience—obedience to all that the ages have proved, obedience to all that the Lord has commanded, and obedience to all those finer things that men already know in their inmost hearts.

❀ ❀ ❀

PEACE is a positive, and not merely a passive, thing. Peace is more than mere absence of war. It is a mode of living, a state of well-being, a condition of self-control and social balance, in which the honest labor of each man contributes to the creation of desirable things. It is that manner of living in which we enjoy the warm fellowship of friends and neighbors, and in which each man finds no accusation directed toward his conscience from within his own soul. It is freedom from the confusion of disorderly places, and freedom from the confusion of disorderly thinking. It is that blessed condition of which the Savior spoke when He said: "Peace I leave with you, my peace I give unto you: not as the world giveth, give I unto you. Let not your heart be troubled, neither let it be afraid."[80]

❀ ❀ ❀

SINCE history has been preserved to us, its pages have been colored with the words of prophets, inspired men of God, foretelling an unbroken reign of peace, when the rule of righteousness will cover the face of the earth, and when men will spend their God-given intelligence and wisdom upon the creation of things that make for more abundant living, rather than upon defense, warfare, balance of power, and international intrigue. But the Lord God will force peace upon no man, even with the coming of that promised day. If there be any to

126

whom peace is not worth the price asked for it, they will not have peace in their hearts nor in their thoughts, even though they are forced to maintain an outward semblance of peace.

※ ※ ※

THERE are many conditions of blessedness of which the Lord has spoken through His servants the prophets, including both those which are enumerated in the Sermon on the Mount and those which were given utterance during the centuries before and the generations that have followed the Meridian of Time. But there is one state of blessedness spoken by a prophet of the Most High which has not been so often repeated as some of the others, but which, veritably, can be fervently endorsed both by those who have a quiet conscience and, in a less comfortable way, by those who have not. It is simply this, and it speaks more than the number of its words would lead one to believe it could: "If ye have slept in peace blessed are you."[81]

6. CONCERNING PRAYER

It is good to be self-reliant and to feel within us the power to shape our lives and to make our living conform to the blueprints of our dreams and righteous ambitions. But it is well also to feel with certainty the presence of a Higher Help when life has dealt roughly with us and destroyed some of our cherished plans and frustrated our best efforts. And at such times, men who have learned to pray—and who have made a daily practice of it—find comfort and strength in quiet approach to the Father of us all. But the manner of mortal man's petitioning before the Lord may not well be a prayer of contradiction. That which will give me gain and do my neighbor injury, is not worthy to be asked. That which will please my vanity and destroy humility is not a thing to be sought. "Thy will, not mine be done" is the spirit of a worthy prayer, and it is of those who pray in such manner that the Lord has said: "And it shall come to pass, that before they call, I will answer; and while they are yet speaking, I will hear."[82]

❋ ❋ ❋

"But when ye pray, use not vain repetitions, as the heathen do: for they think that they shall be heard for their much speaking. Be not ye therefore like unto them."[83] And there are still those with us who think they shall be heard for their much speaking, whose only claim to remembrance is their many words.

❋ ❋ ❋

To PRAY is not as though one shouted into a cavern, to hear only the return of his own voice, the echo of his own thoughts. To pray is rather like the quiet and thoughtful communion of friends who speak each to the other with understanding, who discern each the desire of the other, even though they speak not audibly all that comes to mind.

❀ ❀ ❀

ALL men must sometime find need to pray, for there come into the lives of all of us those things which are beyond our power to control or understand, for which we must seek answer beyond the material causes to which we give so much attention.

❀ ❀ ❀

THERE is no loneliness so great, so absolute, so utterly complete, as the loneliness of a man who cannot call upon the Lord. We may surround ourselves with all of the material things that the world has to offer. We may enrich our lives with a circle of congenial friends. We may glory in the warm kinship of family life. But that man who, in his time of need, cannot pray with confidence that he is being heard, is of all men most lonely in a world where there is much loneliness.

❀ ❀ ❀

THE attitude with which men approach the Lord is not greatly different from the attitude with which they approach their fellow men. There are some who, not having earned their daily bread, nevertheless feel free to demand it. Likewise, there are some who, not having kept the commandments of God, nevertheless feel free to expect His blessings, and find rancor in their souls if such blessings are not forthcoming. Even as there are some who rely upon the mercy and generosity of other men rather than on their own deserving, so are there many who needs must ask the Lord to be merciful, rather than just, for justice would not be sufficient for them.

❄ ❄ ❄

HE WHO has ceased to pray has lost a great friendship, and he who has never prayed has never known the greatest companionship that can come to mortal man—the companionship of man with his Maker; the understanding between mortal being and God; the loving trust between child and Father.

7. AS MEN REPENT

WE HEAR much about repentance. It is one of the choice gifts of God to men—the means whereby a man who has erred may renew a right spirit within him and may live life again without the peace-destroying accusations of conscience. But sometimes, in our joy that a man has repented, we are led to glorify him more than the man who has not sinned and therefore needs no repentance. Regret for one's misdeeds is a thing to be highly commended. But to refrain from doing those things for which we must later repent is more commendable. If men must regret tomorrow what they have done today, they may be grateful for tomorrow's opportunity to repent; but if men avoid doing those things for which repentance is required, they may use tomorrow for further achievement and not merely for the undoing of today's misdeeds. And, therefore, in the journey of eternity, they who refrain from misconduct find themselves farther along the road than those who must go back to correct the error of their ways.

❀ ❀ ❀

IT IS not enough to walk uprightly before God and with one's fellow men on the Sabbath Day, and then to revert to questionable ways of living between Sabbaths. It is not enough to be generous and honorable at convenient times, only to forget these virtues when they hamper one's convenience. Not by rare and isolated acts of goodness, of generosity, or of service do men become acceptable unto themselves and unto God; but rather by goodness

131

itself—a reservoir of it in the heart, from which comes a constant daily flow. And the man who abuses his own life and tarnishes all he touches, then dies, leaving his money to a good cause when he can no longer enjoy it himself—that man has not made amends for his mistaken ways, for he has neither conquered the evils of self nor sacrificed aught for the good of others. Such death-bed repentance cannot undo the manner of a man's living.

❊ ❊ ❊

To CHOOSE humility is much more becoming to men than to have humility thrust upon them un-invited. The thoughtful and humble attitude of life graces the man of plenty no less than the child of need, and the man of power no less than the impotent. This virtue—humility—visits whom it will. When invited, it is mild and friendly and brings with it peace. But when humility must force itself upon the proud and unyielding, it deals heavy blows in its humbling discipline. It sometimes happens that men behave well because good behavior is forced upon them. Happily, there are also those in great numbers who live commendable lives because they prefer to do so. Concerning these two classes of people the record of scripture says: "Because ye are compelled to be humble blessed are ye; for a man sometimes, if he is compelled to be humble, seeketh repentance; and now surely, whosoever repenteth shall find mercy . . . do ye not suppose that they are more blessed who truly humble themselves . . . without being compelled to be humble? Blessed is he that believeth in the word of God . . . without stubbornness of heart . . . without being compelled to know, before they will believe."[84]

❊ ❊ ❊

THERE are many kinds of repentance, and some are greatly more to be desired than others. There is the repentance that is forced upon us—an outward semblance of something that does not exist within. There is the repentance of convenience. And then there is that repentance born of an honest desire to turn from old ways and to follow the paths of righteousness.

❋ ❋ ❋

THE ideal toward which we strive is that men will live so that none will have need of repentance. But until this as yet unattainable goal is realized, all men have need of daily forgiveness.

❋ ❋ ❋

IF WE find cause for discouragement in the story of humanity, it is because of the frequency with which men, collectively, make the same mistakes— because of the seeming disregard for the lessons of history and the wisdom of generations, and because of the apparent unconcern for the fact that every broken law exacts its penalty. If we find cause for hope in the story of humanity it is because of the frequency with which the degradation of man's own devising brings him to repentance and because of the certainty with which the Lord God extends His forgiveness to those who are repentant—after they have paid the price of their misdoing.

❋ ❋ ❋

BY ALL men may it be remembered that the season for following counsel is before the penalties of neglect must be paid; and the season for heeding the commandments of the Lord God is while there is yet time and life is still upon us.

8. PROPHETS AND PROPHECY

THE cost of being a thinking person is always great. But he who speaks the mind and will of the Lord to the condemnation of the ungodly finds adversity multiplied. It is a task of terrifying proportions, which even men of strength and courage would avoid if they could, to stand out from the crowd and tell onrushing humanity toward what inevitable end it is headed. But this, under divine appointment, is what a prophet must do.

❁ ❁ ❁

CONCERNING the future, there are some things we know and some things we do not know. That which we know, we know in general and not in detail. We do not know whether we shall be at peace or at war a year or a decade hence—but we do know that the words of all of the prophets shall yet be fulfilled. We do not know whether we shall be in poverty or plenty in the seasons and the years to come—but we do know that they who keep the commandments of the Lord God will reap the rewards of obedience, and that they who keep them not will pay some form of penalty for each infraction. We do not know what will be the popular theories of learning; what philosophies will be acclaimed; what scientific discovery will bring forth; nor do we know what the social order will be, nor what political views will hold sway, nor after whom men will be following—but we do know that the fundamental principles of life will remain unchanged and that there is no escape from them and no short-cut to glory.

❁ ❁ ❁

WE FIND ourselves often quoting from the prophets, and lest there be some doubt as to what a prophet is, we submit that a prophet is one who, under the appointment and inspiration of the Lord God, speaks truth as the Spirit moves him, regardless of what the world is thinking, and regardless of what men would like to hear. And, therefore, a prophet is seldom popular, and the cost of being a prophet is always great: for he may be called upon to say those things which are not pleasing, even unto himself; he may find himself fighting against a tide of mass misconception, and, as history records, he may be stoned, crucified, banished, ridiculed or shunned —for the truth is not pleasing unto all men, and time has proved that majorities are not always right. Commenting on the manner in which men are wont to receive the words of prophecy, an ancient American prophet said: "Do not say that I have spoken hard things against you; for if ye do, ye will revile against the truth; for I have spoken the words of your Maker. I know that the words of truth are hard against all uncleanness; but the righteous fear them not, for they love the truth and are not shaken."[85]

❉ ❉ ❉

"AND there shall be a new heaven and a new earth. For all old things shall pass away, and all things shall become new, even the heaven and the earth, and all the fulness thereof. . . . And the righteous shall be gathered on my right hand unto eternal life; and the wicked on my left hand will I be ashamed to own before the Father."[86] Such is the great and ultimate end of all prophecy; such is the day of judgment, compensation, and retribution, toward which the prophets have looked and for which the reformers have reached. Such is the inevitable time of reckoning which, say the scriptures, all men will face, somewhere along the eternal journey.

* * *

IN THIS time of troubled hearts, when one day knoweth not what the next will bring, we come to know with an all-consuming conviction that the world and its strongholds offer no refuge except as we take shelter in those sure words of the Lord God which have been spoken by Him and His prophets down through the ages. Perhaps these promised events do not come when we would like them to. Waiting and postponement are the common lot of all men. If we must wait for permanent peace, it is worth it. If we must wait for righteousness to cover the earth, it is worth it. And blessed of all men is he who can wait with an unwavering faith that no matter what fires we shall be called upon to pass through, there will yet come a day when all men shall receive their reward, whether it be unto good or unto evil. And lest there be those who are fearful of the outcome: "Remember, remember that it is not the work of God that is frustrated, but the work of men."[87]

* * *

THERE is that about the record of prophecy which, even though it may not be pleasant to our ears, strikes conviction to our souls.

* * *

"WHICH of the prophets have not your fathers persecuted?"[88]

VI. Toward Endless Things to Come

"For they shall rest from all their labors here, and shall continue their works."[89]

1. DEATH AND IMMORTALITY

INCREASINGLY as we go through life, we come to know that death is the common lot of all men— not that death which, with finality, consigns men to annihilation, but that death which is at once an ending and a beginning—by which men leave behind the cares of mortality and enter an existence yet more glorious. None of us can avoid it. It comes alike to king and pauper, to the righteous and to the unrighteous. Wherein we differ is not in our ability to avert death, but in the attitude with which we meet it, whether it be unto us or unto those we love. Learning to face death with trust and confidence is one of the greatest triumphs of the soul, and it belongs unto him who can say, when asked whither death will take him: "I go where the love and the mercy and the wisdom of my Father in Heaven wish to take me." Over him who can face it with such serenity, death can hold no terror, and no sorrow beyond the sorrow of a temporary parting. Viewed with such certain faith as this, death becomes merely the last venture of this life and the first great adventure of that life which is to follow.

❋ ❋ ❋

WHEN men have seen the doors of eternity open at the beginning of a new life and close as one whose work is finished has departed upon earth's last journey, scarcely can they doubt that this fleeting time we know as life is neither a beginning nor an ending. Scarcely can they doubt that there will be another meeting in that bright abode toward which

139

our separate journeys are moving as the days and the weeks and the hours pass us by.

❋ ❋ ❋

THERE is no more persistent question in life than that of immortality, and, aside from a universal conviction that men are immortal, perhaps there is no greater witness of its truth than that men deal in futures. Thoughtful men always do some of their living in the future. That time never comes in the life of a man when his planning and his thinking do not extend beyond the present. This is true of those who seemingly yet have far to travel on the journey of life, and also of those who seemingly have not far to go. This universal looking toward things to come, this ever-present awareness of what now lies beyond the consciousness of man, is born of man's certainty of perpetual continuance. No matter what the present realization or past enjoyment, young and old alike look toward things to come, because the soul of man will always live to behold and enjoy things to come.

❋ ❋ ❋

"WHAT man is he that liveth, and shall not see death?"[90] So said a prophet of Israel. Few of us face seriously the inevitable end of our life here, and yet there is nothing so certain as that we shall some time leave these familiar surroundings and pass to another sphere of living reality through the change which men call death. Some fear it; others have glorified and looked forward to it as another of life's experiences which may not be known in any other way than by passing through the portals whence go all men. The conviction that death is a change and not an end, a transition and not a finality, has been the strength of those who have passed serenely to those scenes which we shall all one time behold; and neither the uncertainty of life nor the certainty of death can destroy the peace of those with whom is found such assurance.

* * *

As COMES the close of day with merciful sleep to those who are weary and by toil have earned quiet repose, so comes the end of the journey of life to those whom the years have worn with well-doing and who look toward another place of abode, not with doubts or fears or troubled hearts or restless conscience, but with that peace and assurance which Jesus the Christ gave unto men when He said: "In my Father's house are many mansions: if it were not so, I would have told you. I go to prepare a place for you . . . that where I am, there ye may be also."[91]

* * *

"The spirit and the body are the soul of man."[92]

2. ETERNAL JOURNEY

BRING back our yesterdays? No. Yesterdays are the pleasant opiates of the aged and the tormenters of time's prodigals. There is no greater finality in the world than the record of our yesterdays. But an all-wise Creator has ruled that as surely as our yesterdays have ever been, so surely will our tomorrows be never ending.

❀ ❀ ❀

THE constant beckoning of the limitless unknown urges us on to live, as it always has and always will, no matter what age we have attained as men count time. It is this ceaseless quest, this endless reaching beyond the known into the unknown, that makes men grow, as they always have and always will. The freshness and joy of life are with us always, because never shall we exhaust the thrill of discovery. It is, even as Paul wrote: "Eye hath not seen, nor ear heard, neither have entered into the heart of man, the things which God hath prepared for them that love him."[93] And man, an eternal being, with an illimitable future, finds himself forever reaching beyond the present into the realm of the unknown.

❀ ❀ ❀

WHILE the Fatherhood of God and the brotherhood of man are literal realities, they are usually given only theoretical or idealistic values in our thinking and our living. But, when we are honest with ourselves and straight in our thinking, we come to the realization that many of the barriers that rise between brother and brother are relatively superficial when viewed in terms of an eternal journey. And, while our training and acquired habits of thinking may make such differences seem to be fundamental, the fact is that we have more in common with all other men than we suppose. Consider, for example, that gulf which lies between him who is academically informed and him who is not. There is so much of which we are all ignorant that it would seem our common ignorance is a greater common denominator than the difference between our ignorance and our knowledge. Then, too, the man who is an authority in one field is so often innocent of reliable knowledge in so many other fields, which again lessens the fundamental difference between him and the man who is totally uninformed. And, except for the occasional special endowments of genius, and for occasional mental incapacity, the difference between the greatest and the least of us in the field of acquired knowledge is a few years of study and research. In the brotherhood of man such differences are not fundamental, and the plan of life and salvation which the Savior of the world left for our guidance may surmount all such superficial barriers as men pursue their eternal journey.

❋ ❋ ❋

WE HEAR many complain of unfinished work, of too much to be done, of days that are overly busy. Such complaining is a human trait, as old as the ages, but before adding our voices to the complaining chorus, each of us should consider well the immeasurable blessing that lies in the fact that our work is never done. When all has been accomplished, our usefulness will have passed. But so long as there is work to do—so long as there are aims to achieve, goals to reach, and worlds to conquer— happiness is yet possible to men. God grant that we may never be left without work to do—either here or hereafter.

* * *

Men have in common a love of life, even under conditions which make love of life difficult to understand. Starving millions would rather live than die. The infirm cling to their ailing days, and even when interest has been lost in the values of this world, the eternal values and man's own consciousness of his immortality make it good to be alive in a transitory existence that moves rapidly toward an infinite goal.

* * *

Nothing that men do is, or can ever be, entirely dissociated from all other things that men do. No single act of our lives is ever performed without some preface of circumstance, without some reason, even though that reason may not be a good one. The last step down is merely another step that has been preceded by many steps in the same direction. The highest step up is simply another step attained by having climbed up countless other steps in the same direction. And since every act and deed and thought has its preface and its sequel in other acts and deeds and thoughts, it profiteth a man to make sure that every act and deed and thought of his life contributes to an endless progression in the right direction.

* * *

Men find themselves searching for things that endure: principles that will not have to be abandoned tomorrow; ideals that are good as long as time will last; friendships that continue to the grave and beyond; truths that are truths rather than vain sup-

144

position; and eternal realities that will last far beyond the limits of this life.

* * *

THE heavens are telling the glory of God, and all
creation stands witness to the wonder of His work.
Seasons come and go, years roll by, centuries pass,
and ages fade into the dim distant past, while life
and truth go on forever—but this day and hour in
which we live is as surely a part of eternity as will
be another day and hour a hundred or a thousand
years hence.

* * *

ONE of the most universal attributes of human
nature is the manner in which we feel ourselves
immune to the ills to which all other men fall heir.
A man in good health may be led to suppose that
he will always enjoy good health—no matter how
he lives or what has been the experience of others.
A man with a steady income and an accumulation
of wealth may be led to suppose that these things
are assured unto him perpetually. We see all manner of calamity befalling countless other men but
seldom seriously think of ourselves in the place of
those who have been brought low, until sorrow presents itself at our door. It is generally true even
with death itself: Other men may die young—other
men may be cut short long before they are prepared
—but surely not us. And so we go on living our lives
with a self-assurance, untenable albeit universal.
And out of these thoughts there comes this fervent
wish: May God help every man to set his house in
order while yet he may—help him to live each day
as a vitally important part of an eternal journey.

* * *

IT IS within the experience of all men to seem to remember things that lie beyond the reach of memory—to seem to recall things that are beyond recall. Flashes of recollection momentarily light up experiences of the past that are familiar, yet not familiar. Perhaps at such times we approach nearer unto the truth concerning a life before this we now live and a life beyond the certain end that we now see. It is this presentiment of things which lie beyond our present reach and understanding that causes men to accept life as a time of preparation for greater things that lie beyond. It is these things, and what may be their import, that are the subject of a hymn which world-wide visitors to Temple Square often hear sung by the choir and played by the organ. It is a hymn that speaks of a previous personal existence of man, a probationary present in a brief but important school of life, and an illimitable hereafter wherein men will find themselves eternally progressing and will find continued existence under circumstances determined by the deeds and the thoughts and the usefulness of the life they now live. It speaks also of a Heavenly Father and an Eternal Mother, and is known by the title, "O My Father":

> O my Father, Thou that dwellest
> In the high and glorious place!
> When shall I regain Thy presence,
> And again behold Thy face?
> In Thy holy habitation,
> Did my spirit once reside;
> In my first primeval childhood,
> Was I nurtured near Thy side?
>
> For a wise and glorious purpose
> Thou hast placed me here on earth,

And withheld the recollection
Of my former friends and birth,
Yet ofttimes a secret something
Whispered, "You're a stranger here";
And I felt that I had wandered
From a more exalted sphere.

I had learned to call Thee Father,
Through Thy Spirit from on high,
But, until the Key of Knowledge
Was restored I knew not why.
In the heavens are parents single?
No, the thought makes reason stare!
Truth is reason; Truth eternal
Tells me I've a mother there.

When I leave this frail existence,
When I lay this mortal by,
Father, Mother, may I meet you,
In your royal courts on high?
Then at length, when I've completed
All you sent me forth to do,
With your mutual approbation
Let me come and dwell with you.[94]

❋ ❋ ❋

"Man was also in the beginning with God."[95]

Appendix

REFERENCES TO QUOTED PASSAGES

1. Psalm 121: 1-3.
2. Job 7: 6.
3. Doctrine & Covenants 124: 86.
4. Genesis 28: 16.
5. Proverbs 4: 5, 7.
6. Doctrine & Covenants 78: 10.
7. Doctrine & Covenants 130: 18, 19.
8. Galatians 6: 7.
9. Rev. 13: 9-10.
10. Doctrine & Covenants 76: 22-24.
11. Book of Mormon—II Nephi 9: 28.
12. Matthew 7: 3.
13. Book of Mormon—II Nephi 9: 28, 29.
14. John 7: 23.
15. Ecclesiastes 8: 11-13.
16. Proverbs 4: 26, 27.
17. Job 7: 4.
18. Psalm 127: 1.
19. Isaiah 51: 12, 13.
20. Genesis 1: 2-5.
21. Psalm 51: 9, 10.
22. Doctrine & Covenants 88: 91.
23. Doctrine & Covenants 88: 42, 45, 47.
24. Job 38: 2, 17, 19, 34-36.
25. Ecclesiastes 5: 8; 12: 13.
26. Doctrine & Covenants 101: 7, 8.
27. Exodus 20: 8-10.
28. Exodus 20: 17.
29. Proverbs 13: 11.
30. Proverbs 28: 19.
31. Psalm 37: 25.
32. Book of Mormon—Alma 60: 20.
33. 2 Peter 2: 19.
34. Doctrine & Covenants 130: 20, 21.
35. Book of Mormon—Ether 2: 12.

36. Doctrine & Covenants 98: 8-10.
37. Doctrine & Covenants 88: 86
38. Book of Mormon—Alma 60: 20.
39. Doctrine & Covenants 88: 34, 35.
40. I Kings 19: 11, 12.
41. *Joseph Smith.*
42. Doctrine & Covenants 101: 80.
43. Doctrine & Covenants 134: 1, 2.
44. Doctrine & Covenants 59: 23.
45. Doctrine & Covenants 3: 2.
46. Book of Mormon—Alma 29: 5; Moroni 7: 15.
47. Book of Mormon—Mosiah 29: 26, 27.
48. Book of Mormon—II Nephi 9: 25.
49. Doctrine & Covenants 131: 6.
50. *The Inn Album*—Canto 5.
51. *Johnson.*
52. Doctrine & Covenants 58: 26-29.
53. Proverbs 12: 19.
54. Doctrine & Covenants 88: 66.
55. Matthew 6: 7.
56. Ecclesiastes 5: 3.
57. Book of Mormon—II Nephi 33: 6.
58. Doctrine & Covenants 1: 2, 4, 10.
59. Book of Mormon—I Nephi 17: 50.
60. Matthew 6: 4.
61. Proverbs 30: 8.
62. Luke 12: 48.
63. Exodus 20: 7.
64. Adapted from Luke 21 and Doctrine & Covenants 45 and 88.
65. Psalm 46: 10.
66. Doctrine & Covenants 3: 6-8; 122: 9.
67. Nehemiah 9: 6.
68. Doctrine & Covenants 20: 17.
69. I John 4: 20.
70. Romans 2: 6.
71. Doctrine & Covenants 56: 16, 17.
72. Book of Mormon—Alma 9: 13.
73. Psalm 37: 1-3, 16.
74. Psalm 30: 6.
75. Doctrine & Covenants 68: 25, 28.
76. Book of Mormon—Alma 37: 35-36.
77. *Joseph Smith.*
78. Mark 15: 34.

79. Luke 19: 42.
80. John 14: 27.
81. Doctrine & Covenants 45: 46.
82. Isaiah 65: 24.
83. Matthew 6: 7-8.
84. Adapted from Book of Mormon—Alma 32: 13-16.
85. Book of Mormon—II Nephi 9: 40.
86. Doctrine & Covenants 29: 23, 24, 27.
87. Doctrine & Covenants 3: 3.
88. Acts 7: 52.
89. Doctrine & Covenants 124: 86.
90. Psalm 89: 48.
91. John 14: 2, 3.
92. Doctrine & Covenants 88: 15.
93. I Corinthians 2: 9.
94. *Eliza R. Snow.*
95. Doctrine & Covenants 93: 29.